YOU'RE ONLY YOUNG ONCE!

by

PETER GRAYSTONE

PAUL SHARPE

PIPPA TURNER

Group Bible study
for over 13s

Scripture Union
130 City Road, London EC1V 2NJ

YOU'RE ONLY YOUNG ONCE! has been developed in the
Education in Churches department of Scripture Union, and may
be used alongside the 'Learning Together' scheme of
education and worship in churches.

© Scripture Union 1992
First published 1992

ISBN 0 86201 751 3

British Library Cataloguing in Publication Data
A catalogue record of this book is available from the British
Library.

Cover design by Ross Advertising and Design Ltd.
Book design by Tony Cantale Graphics.

All Scripture quotations are taken from the *Good News Bible*.
Old Testament: copyright © American Bible Society 1976. New
Testament: copyright © American Bible Society 1966, 1971,
1976.

Printed and bound in Great Britain by Ebenezer Baylis and Son
Ltd, The Trinity Press, Worcester and London.

CONTENTS

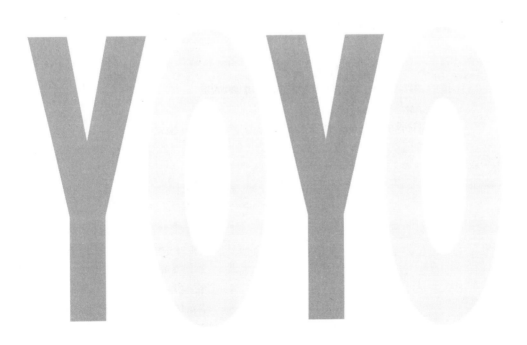

AND THERE'S MORE!

Books 2, 3 and 4 of YOU'RE ONLY YOUNG ONCE! will be available (as they are published through '92 and '93) where you bought this volume.

BOOK 2

1 Friendship
2 Parents
3 Girlfriends and boyfriends
4 Sex
5 Being alone
6 Prejudice and racism
7 What is church for?
8 A living God (suitable for Easter)

BOOK 3

1 Why am I here?
2 Self worth
3 Can't be bothered
4 Getting your priorities right
5 Exploiting God's creation
6 Attitudes to the developing world
7 Suffering
8 God within me (suitable for Pentecost)

BOOK 4

1 What is God like?
2 Reasons for believing
3 What does God expect of me?
4 Where's my life going?
5 Endings and beginnings
6 Prayer
7 The Bible
8 Doubt

YOU'RE ONLY YOUNG ONCE!?

One of the difficulties of choosing material to use in a church setting with young people is that there are so many different kinds of group that no single scheme fits every situation. YOYO! has been devised in the hope that it will meet the needs of more groups than any other scheme. It has a thematic format and every theme is worked through in three distinct ways. Most churches will find that one of the three approaches comes fairly close to fitting their requirements as it stands. Others will find that the ideas are laid out in such a straightforward way that they can mix and match, using one of the three approaches as a basis.

APPROACH 1: INVESTIGATOR

This approach assumes that the teenagers taking part come from a wide range of stages of faith. Typically, some may have grown up in Christian families and progressed through the church's children's groups, others may be their friends who have little experience of Christianity in their background and attend the group for social reasons, some may have a maturing faith, while others have attended the church by habit but never personalised their commitment, and of course, some may sincerely want to argue against Christian beliefs.

There is a good deal of discussion in this approach, in which committed Christians can put their points of view alongside those whose interest in the gospel is slim. The themes are examined from many angles, but the Bible is consistently used to show that God has an opinion on whatever subject is under discussion. Although Scripture is studied in each programme, group members will not be expected to have brought a Bible with them – the passages they are asked to consider are either read to them or given in photocopied form. Prayer and praise are used in ways which allow participants to take part honestly, or to observe without feeling under pressure to involve themselves. Each programme is designed to last for sixty fast-moving minutes.

APPROACH 2: PIONEER

This is for use as a short epilogue or introduction to a club the main function of which is recreational. It makes no assumptions that the participants have a Christian commitment of any depth. Although the Bible is at the heart of each programme, it is not taken for granted that the teenagers will accept it as relevant to their lives – nor is it assumed that they have a particular desire to attend this part of the session. The activities are therefore attention-grabbing, and a very brief talk sometimes prompts a short discussion. This group is rarely required to pray (which would appear meaningless to non-believers). The programme lasts about ten minutes.

APPROACH 3: *CHALLENGER*

The third approach assumes that all its participants mean business with God and want to put themselves under the authority of the Bible as a guide for their lifestyles. It encourages them to discover how to interpret the Bible intelligently and apply its principles sensitively.

The young people will usually need access to a Bible each for in-depth study. This study, however, takes the form of creative exploration, rather than a traditional list of questions to which a 'correct' answer can be found. Basic doctrinal teaching is followed each time by discussion activities about what their practical response should be. The imaginative approaches to prayer and praise make the assumption that those taking part have a faith which they want to express. The programmes are timed at sixty minutes, but this is best regarded as a minimum so as to allow Bible studies and discussions to develop at their own pace.

MIX AND MATCH?

Because no single group of young people is likely to fall exclusively into one of the three categories, it is understood that some youth groups will find themselves mixing and matching activities from the three approaches. It is recommended that, in this case, one approach is used as a structure from which activities can be swapped, omitted or added to.

LEADERSHIP. YOYO! is designed to be used with groups from seven or eight in number up to a very substantial size. Many of the activities take place in subgroups of four or five, with young people working by themselves. It is envisaged that one adult or older teenage leader will run the programme, with other leaders in supporting roles (taking part in sketches, distributing materials, giving a talk or instructions for an activity, encouraging the subgroups as they take part, finding opportunities to develop relationships) in a suitable ratio to the size of the group.

CHOOSING AN APPROACH. On the basis of the information given in the previous section, choose which approach best suits the teenagers you are seeking to attract to the meeting. Some churches, of course, have different groups of teenagers meeting at different times and will want to use two or three of the approaches to the same theme during any one week. If a mix-and-match approach is being used, make the selection carefully so that it includes Bible teaching, application and (except with unchurched youngsters) prayer with equal prominence.

TALKS. Bear in mind that this material is for group Bible study. It is designed to give maximum participation to the group members, and the talks have deliberately been kept short, giving only sufficient basic doctrinal teaching to ensure that the Bible study and discussions which follow have a secure foundation. Although Bible references are given so that the leaders will have confidence in the authority of what they are saying, reading them in context, not simply as proof texts, it is not necessary to read these to the group unless there is a particular reason for stressing the message of one of them. Some advice to the leaders who give these talks:

✔ Try not to exceed the time allocated, which is the appropriate length for a non-visual presentation to young people.

✔ Choose the parts of the notes that seem most punchy, and stress those.

✔ Do not read verbatim from the book; prepare your talk by writing the points you want to make on a postcard.

✔ Rehearse it well enough to be able to deliver the talk using the card only as a memory-jogger.

✔ If a brief illustration from your personal experience comes to mind, this will have a greater impact than making a more abstract point.

✔ You cannot preach an entire sermon in five minutes; be content with saying a little, but saying it memorably.

ACTIVITIES. Resist the temptation to force the group members to come to a pre-ordained conclusion during discussion activities. During activities which involve creative work, discussion or Bible study, the groups should be left to make their own decisions. The role of the leaders is to give clear, well-practised instructions, then to act as encouragers, providers of materials and time-keepers. It is appropriate for leaders to sit in on groups, since these are good occasions to develop relationships, but they should make it obvious that they are participants in the activity, not directors of it. In the same way, prayer activities should involve group-members forming their own honest responses to God as much as possible. The leaders should go home at the end of the session not necessarily having seen their mainstream Christian viewpoint demolish all alternatives, but content that a godly point of view has been put in a relevant way. The rest is the Holy Spirit's work!

CHAPTER 1

WHY ARE CHRISTIANS SO BORING? 1

WHAT'S THE BIG IDEA?

Many teenagers are embarrassed to go to Christian meetings, not because they are unsympathetic to the faith, but because they do not want to be identified with the stereotype of people who go to church. This programme examines the image that Christians present and challenges the notion that Christians must be boring. It is a low-key introductory session, emphasising involvement and fun, rather than the serious study of later programmes.

PRINCIPAL BIBLE PASSAGE
PHILIPPIANS 1:27—2:4

MAJOR POINTS THAT CAN BE MADE

▼ Jesus' lifestyle was adventurous, rebellious, anything but boring – however, he was first and foremost obedient to God.

OTHER PASSAGES USED
NEHEMIAH 5:15, MARK 12:41–44, LUKE 1:26–38; 5:29–31; 7:36–39, 44–48; 18:18–23, JOHN 2:13–17, ACTS 5:40–42; 9:32–35, 2 CORINTHIANS 11:23–29, PHILIPPIANS 2:15–16

▼ Christians are called to reflect this attractive lifestyle, just as the Christians of the early church did.

▼ The onus is on Christians to impress non-believers by the joy and fulfilment they show.

▼ Do you dare to be different?

APPROACH 1: INVESTIGATOR

1 WILD GAME (10 minutes)

Play a zany game which could not possibly be considered boring. For example, split the group into teams, each with a camera and a suit of ludicrous clothes (eg a floppy hat, waistcoat, ballet tutu and wellingtons). In relay, everyone runs across the room, dresses, has his or her photograph taken, rips the clothes off and runs back. Declare a winning team and have the photographs developed for display next week.

RESOURCES
'NOW I'M A CHRISTIAN...', JIM SMITH, SCRIPTURE UNION

2 CONTRASTS (5 minutes)

Give out photocopies of the list of contrasts on page 14. The group should, individually, mark a cross (X) on the line to indicate which of the pair more closely resembles an aspect of their own personality. (The cross need not go at one extreme or the opposite; it could go in the middle or nearer one end than the other.) Having completed that, they go through the list again, marking a circle (o) on the line to indicate where they feel most Christians give the impression of being. The circle will be on top of the cross when they think they are very like this stereotype of Christians in a particular characteristic, but the marks will be wide apart when they want to distance themselves from what they perceive Christians to be like.

Suggest that they quickly make a gut reaction, rather than agonising over the precise meaning of these metaphors. Put the sheets on one side to refer to later.

3 SKETCH AND DISCUSSION (20 minutes)

This sketch depends for its success on the ability of the person playing Raz Kane to open up the sketch into a discussion. Raz Kane, wearing a long raincoat and carrying a microphone, roves the room addressing questions to people sitting around. To begin with, these answers have been rehearsed (simply give certain people pieces of paper ten minutes before the meeting telling them roughly what to say). At the end of the sketch, the interviewer should seamlessly turn it into a discussion by asking similar questions of others, who have not had their answers prepared.

Raz Kane: This is Raz Kane, roving reporter, coming to you live from a youth group that occasionally, I am told, attempts to address Christian issues. Right here, right now, I'm going to try to get to the base of the problem: Why are Christians so boring? I hope to discover the answer to such as yet unfathomed mysteries as: Why are Christian unions all over the country filled with the most boring people in the school? What is it about 1970s haircuts and Songs of Praise that attracts middle-aged Christians? Why can so many young Christians be recognised instantly by their stone washed jeans and acrylic jumpers? *(Raz picks out the first of the rehearsed contributors in the room and goes to interview him.)* This looks like an intelligent man. You sir, would you mind answering a few questions? Are you a Christian?

1st Actor: Yes.

Raz Kane: Would you say you were boring?

1st Actor: No.

2nd Actor: *(Interrupts)* You pigging well are!

1st Actor: No, I'm not.

2nd Actor: All right then, why wouldn't you come to Ray's video party last Saturday night?

1st Actor: Er, well... I... it was my sister's birthday and this meal had been arranged for ages.

2nd Actor: Lying toad! You said last Thursday that you were coming.

1st Actor: Did I? Oh well... yeah but that was before I heard it was going to be... I mean... er... I forgot.

2nd Actor: Forgot what, the party?

1st Actor: No, my sister's birthday. *(Argument continues as Raz Kane moves to next actor.)*

Raz Kane: Well there seems to be some sort of disagreement there. I'm moving now towards the door. You, sir, are you prepared to answer some questions? Why are Christians so boring?

3rd Actor: I dunno. They never want to do anything. It's not really their fault. It's coz of all those rules they have to follow. Can't drink, can't smoke, can't have girlfriends (well, not proper ones), can't go to parties, that kind of thing.

Raz Kane: *(To next person)* Do you have an opinion on Christians?

4th Actor: They're all clones aren't they? The trouble with Christians is that they can't think for themselves. That's why they're so boring. They all do the same things because they are all following the same rules.

Raz Kane: Are you a Christian?

4th Actor: No way! People who are boring become Christians. That's all right for some people if they need direction. Anyone with a bit of flair doesn't need to believe in God. It's people without imagination that get drawn towards religion. That's why Christians are boring.

Raz Kane: Thank you sir. Most provocative! Has anyone been provoked? *(Raz Kane makes questioning eye contact with as many people as possible as a stimulus to get others prepared to discuss. He moves to another person, who pretends that he wasn't expecting the question.)* Why are Christians so boring?

5th Actor: Er... Christians aren't boring. You can't generalise like that. There are boring people in every walk of life, some of them happen to be Christians.

Raz Kane: Isn't that just conveniently avoiding the issue?

5th Actor: No not at all; I'm not boring. If people want to stereotype Christians that's up to them. Why should we care what others think of us?

6th Actor: *(Interrupting)* O come on, that's ridiculous. I wouldn't be seen dead at a Christian meeting with that lot at my school, let alone invite my friends.

5th Actor: That's true, but I do think that unless we try to do something about it we're only bolstering the fake image we've been given.

Raz Kane: Hmm, interesting... but how would you go about doing something about it?

6th Actor: Well... er... well, instead of having Christian meetings to discuss yawn subjects, they should deal with issues that really need talking about. Like 'Why do Christians always have to be in bed by eleven when everyone else is allowed to stay up?' Or 'Is there any chance of talking about God at an acid party?' Something like that...

At this point, the interviewer should feel confident to draw people without prepared answers into the discussion. He may like to ask someone whether they felt that 'dressing up' Christian discussions in such a way would be a compromise, or to what extent Christians invite their own stereotyping. As the discussion continues, ask why it is that sincere Christians are often mocked, and whether the images that have been associated with Christians are fair. Refer to the 'Contrasts' sheet that the group have filled in. Was anyone surprised by the similarities between their assessment of themselves and that of Christians? Or the differences? Focus on some of them that seem relevant to your group - for example, how do Christians rate for adventurousness (Rollercoaster?). Kindness and faithfulness (Mother Teresa?). Are they living in a dream world or too good to be true (Snow White?). Or perhaps Christians are just ordinary – should they be?

4 BIBLE PERSPECTIVE (15 minutes)

Split the group into subgroups of three or four. Give each subgroup eight paper cups (or envelopes or cartons or anything that will hold slips of paper). Each subgroup also needs a felt marker and eight pieces of paper, each bearing one of the names:

Paul	***Jesus***
Peter	***Woman***
Rich man	***The apostles***
Widow	***Mary***

Ask them to write a caption on each cup so that they represent these qualities:

Boring	***Rebellious***
Ordinary	***Laid back***
Heroic	***Obedient***
Soft	***Religious***

Read out the following Bible passages about the eight characters on the slips of paper. After each, the subgroup must talk together and decide, on the basis of what they have heard, which category each character could best be placed in. They put the slip in their chosen cup. Point out that there is not necessarily a 'correct' answer, and that they do not have to put one slip in each cup – any combination is valid as long as it is honest. These are the Bible readings:

2 Corinthians 11:23-29 (Paul)
John 2:13-17 (Jesus)
Acts 9:32-35 (Peter)
Luke 7:36-39,44-48 (Woman)
Luke 18:18-23 (Rich man)
Acts 5:40-42 (The apostles)
Mark 12:41-44 (Widow)
Luke 1:26-38 (Mary)

After the exercise, ask the teenagers to say where they have put most of their papers. Were they surprised by the results? Was there any disagreement? How has it affected their opinion of Jesus and the first Christians?

5 TALK (5 minutes)

Make these points:

✖ The first Christians saw their faith as an adventure, a challenge, a revolution – anything except boring!

✖ Jesus was 'a rebel with a cause'. He refused to be respectable – he went to parties with prostitutes, not because he wanted sex, but because he cared for people who were despised. He refused to get hung up over money – it was the rich man who turned down Jesus' challenge who comes over as a wimp. Jesus refused to do what people expected of him – overturning merchants' tables because he knew they disgraced God.

✖ It's daring to be a Christian, because it means overturning middle-aged 'respectability', overturning middle-class 'money-is-everything' attitudes, and overturning middle-of-the-road 'I've got to be like everyone else' drabness.

✖ There's a danger of Christians stereotyping themselves. It is joy that God has called us to! Let Christians show they can be joyful without being disobedient to God. It's freedom that God has called us to! Let Christians show that they can live out freedom without abusing it.

✖ It is up to Christians to prove they are not boring – to stand out in a crowd because they are seen to have better values, better friendship to offer, and better fun.

✖ Nehemiah in the Old Testament said: 'I acted differently because I honoured God' (5:15). Dare to be different?

6 PRAYER (5 minutes)

Ask the group to write three things on the back of their 'Contrasts' sheets. These are private and will not be shared. They are to scribble down the development that is 'The most exciting thing that could happen...'

✔ ***... in my leisure time.***
✔ ***... in my relationships.***
✔ ***... in my spiritual life.***

Then ask them to consider what God would say about the three things they have written. They are to tick any which God would welcome, cross any which would hurt God, and put a question mark against any which they are not sure about. The leader should say a prayer asking God to fulfil the ones which have been ticked.

APPROACH 2: *PIONEER*

1 *IS IT TRUE?* (2 minutes)
Give out photocopies of page 15, a list of answers to the question: 'Do you think Christians are boring?' given by teenagers. Invite the group to read the comments and decide whether they are fair. Is there one which represents their own opinion?

2 *DISCUSSION* (5 minutes)
Ask the members of the group to turn to the person next to them and tell him or her whether they were able to choose one. Then open the question to the whole group for discussion. Do only boring people become Christians? If so, is it the people who are boring, or the things they do – for instance, church services and prayer? Do Christians make good friends? Do those you know who are committed to following Jesus seem to be having fun?

3 *TALK* (3 minutes)
Make these points:

✔ *'Gentle Jesus meek and mild' is a yawn. Was Jesus really as boring as that?*

✔ *He was a 'rebel with a cause' – he knew that God hated the use of the Temple as a market place where traders could make a fast buck out of those who wanted to worship God, but he didn't write a letter to the authorities about it; instead he rioted, overturned the tables, and let the animals loose.*

✔ *He was adventurous – a regular party-goer, Jesus was just as happy socialising with crooks and hookers as with religious leaders.*

✔ *He was obedient – he was able to be totally un-boring without being immoral because he was perfectly obedient to God as his priority.*

✔ *Christians are trying to copy a lifestyle which is rebellious against society's worst values, adventurous instead of being on the money/sex/holidays treadmill, and obedient to the most powerful force in the universe. Dare to be different?*

(John 2:13-16, Luke 5:29-30, Philippians 2:8)

APPROACH 3: *CHALLENGER*

1 *DISCUSSION* (15 minutes)
Give out photocopies of page 15, a list of answers to the question: 'Do you think Christians are boring?' Explain that all the statements were made by people who did not have a Christian faith. Do the group think that the comments are, firstly, true and, secondly, fair? Do any of the Christians present think that their own lifestyle is boring? Why do they think that the idea of following Christ leaves people cold?

2 *BIBLE STUDY* (15 minutes)
Someone should read Philippians 1:27- 2:4. The group splits into pairs. Ask each pair to make a list of all the things Paul tells Christians that they should be doing,and which are listed or hinted at in these verses. After a few minutes, the leader asks them to call out the things they have discovered, and displays a combined list.

Back in pairs, the teenagers should go through the list, giving each item a 'boring factor' from 0 to 10. The ones which the world outside the Christian family would consider to be utterly boring things to be asked to do score 0; the ones which are daring, exciting or challenging get 10. When this has been done, ask the pairs to report back and gauge the amount of agreement on the scores.

Talk about the high scorers. How can we display the excitement of these features of Christian life in ways which would prove attractive to those who do not share our faith?

Then discuss the low scorers. Why have they scored low? Why does God ask these things of us? Is there any virtue in them to which others could warm?

3 TALK (5 minutes)

Read Philippians 2:15-16, then make these points:

✎ As Christians we are called to be different. However, the image of 'stars in the night sky' is one of dazzle and brilliance. Paul doesn't tell us to be black holes in a glittering galaxy. The onus is on us to show ourselves not to be drab.

✎ As stars, though, we are expected to be 'innocent, pure... perfect'. We are not to be sparkling people at the expense of our obedience. Jesus was compelling and adventurous, but also obedient to what God wanted (2:8).

✎ We must be attractive people because we have 'the message of life' to offer to those who have not discovered the joy of faith in Christ.

Reassure each member of the group: 'You're a star!'

4 POSTER MAKING (15 minutes)

Ask each pair to join another pair and give them a large sheet of paper and some felt-tipped pens. They are to design a poster in the style of a cowboy 'wanted man' poster. It should appeal for Christians to show virtues which display them as attractive and exciting people, but also obedient. The poster should have on it somewhere the words 'Wanted! Christians who are...'. They may complete it, though, with any words and pictures that seem appropriate - trendy, friendly, generous, etc.

5 PRAYER (10 minutes)

As part of their worship each group presents their poster to the rest, explaining why they have chosen particular words and pictures. Display the posters round the walls. Have a time of silence during which the group may invite God to challenge them about anything in their lifestyle which he wants them to change, as they look at the posters. Then have an open time of prayer concerning the friendship, image and influence of the group among non-believers.

6 MEDITATION (5 minutes)

Close with a meditation in which the group is invited to consider Jesus' example in these matters. The leader should read Philippians 2:5-11, pausing after each verse for about 30 seconds so that all can form a mental picture of Jesus fulfilling the qualities that are talked of in that phrase.

CONTRASTS

Put a X on the line, somewhere between the two extremes, to indicate how you see yourself and your lifestyle.

Put a O on the line to indicate what you think most Christians are like.

For example, are you more like...?

Action man _____ **Cuddly toy**

CHOOSE:

James Bond _____ **Postman Pat**

Rowing boat on a quiet river _____ **Rollercoaster at Disneyland**

A faithful friend _____ **A rocky romance**

Bart Simpson _____ **Snow White**

Exploring in the exotic East _____ **Two weeks slobbing in Benidorm**

Mother Teresa _____ **Jack the Ripper**

Watching football _____ **Playing football**

MacDonalds yet again _____ **Cooking a new recipe**

T-shirt and jeans _____ **Posh suit**

Honeysuckle _____ **Cactus**

Cool, snazzy boxers _____ **Grandpa's grubby long johns**

Do you think Christians are **BORING?**

We put this question to the people waiting at a bus stop outside a London school.

NO, NOT REALLY. IT'S JUST DOING WHAT THEY THINK IS RIGHT AND I DON'T MIND. IT'S UP TO THEM.

THEY DON'T DO EXCITING THINGS AND IT'S ALL GOING BY LOADS OF RULES, LIKE ALL THE BIBLE... THEY CAN'T DO ANYTHING LIKE DO SOMETHING THEY'RE NOT SUPPOSED TO ONCE IN A WHILE.

BORING? PROBABLY! I DON'T KNOW ANY.

THEY'RE JUST THE SAME AS ANY OTHER PERSON ... THERE'S LOTS OF BORING PEOPLE.

THEY DON'T WANT ANYTHING TO DO WITH US... LIKE IT'S ALL JESUS, JESUS, JESUS.

I'VE GOT THIS FRIEND. WELL HE'S NOT A FRIEND BUT I KNOW HIM. HE'S ALWAYS SAYING, "COME TO CHURCH WITH ME" AND STUFF. BUT EVERYONE SAYS HE'S GAY.

THERE'S NO FUN IN IT. THEY OUGHT TO BE OUT DOING USEFUL THINGS LIKE HELPING OLD PEOPLE AND CLUBS FOR CHILDREN. BUT CHURCH IS JUST LONG... TALKING LONG.

IT'S ALL GOING ON WITH STUFF YOU DON'T UNDERSTAND.

YOU'RE NOT ALLOWED TO HAVE FUN, ARE YOU? ... BOYS AND THAT!

NOT BORING, BUT... IT'S ALWAYS TALKING ABOUT DEATH. IT SEEMS SOMEHOW MORBID.

BUS STOP

CHAPTER 2

WHO IS JESUS?

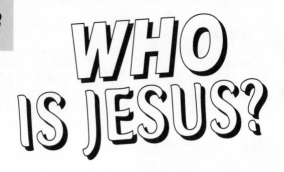

WHAT'S THE BIG IDEA?

This programme moves forward from chapter 1 by examining in more detail the character and qualities of Christ, on whom Christians are seeking to model their lifestyle. It assumes knowledge that Jesus existed – although the extent of the teenagers' knowledge may vary. For some he may be no more than the subject of a swearword; others may have had a lifelong exposure to the stories of his earthly life. Jesus is revealed as a man who claimed that he was God. Is it conceivable that this is true?

PRINCIPAL BIBLE PASSAGE
LUKE 5:1-11

MAJOR POINTS THAT CAN BE MADE

✔ Many accept Jesus as a great and compassionate teacher. However, Christians believe in his perfection, divinity, resurrection and present glory. He claimed these things for himself. Was he telling the truth?

✔ Jesus was in every way a human, and in every way God. If Jesus had only been loving and courageous, he could be of no use to us, except as one more good example.

✔ Because Jesus is ascended and alive, we may make a relationship with him – with friendship, because he was a human like us, but also with awe and awareness of our unworthiness, because he is the holy God.

OTHER PASSAGES USED
EXODUS 3:14, MATTHEW 1:23; 2:1; 4:13; 7:28-29; 9:35-36; 14:25-33; 17:22-23, MARK 1:10-11; 6:3; 8:27-29; 9:2-7, LUKE 2:6,21,46-47,51-52; 4:15, JOHN 8:58; 20:16, ACTS 2:22-24,33, 2 CORINTHIANS 5:21, COLOSSIANS 1:15-19; 2:9; 3:1, HEBREWS 4:15, 1 PETER 2:22-23

APPROACH 1: INVESTIGATOR

1 QUIZ (10 minutes)

Divide the group into up to six subgroups, depending on the number present. Give each subgroup a copy of the multiple choice quiz 'Not so trivial pursuit', on page 22. They are to decide among themselves what the most likely answer is to each question.

RESOURCES
'JESUS 2000', DICK FRANCE et alia, LION.

When all have finished, the quiz begins. Number the groups from 1 to 6. Throw a dice and give the group whose number comes up the first chance to answer the first question. If they are correct, they get two points; if they are wrong, the question passes to the team on their left for a bonus point. Repeat this for each question (if there are two groups they have three numbers each, if there are three

they have two numbers, and so on). Declare a winner.

The answers are : 1b, 2c, 3c, 4b, 5a, 6b, 7c, 8c.

2 TALK (5 minutes)

Use this time to comment on some of the reasons behind those names being given to Jesus, but do not be tempted to dwell on every one listed in the quiz.

In the years before Jesus, the Jews were waiting for a unique king who would drive out the occupying forces and establish a completely fair and peaceful kingdom. They called this longed-for person 'Messiah' or 'Christ' (they mean exactly the same).

When Mary gave birth, the boy was given the name Jesus, which was quite a common name. 'Christ' was not his surname, but as people came to recognise that Jesus was this expected Messiah-king, they began to call him Jesus the Christ (Mark 8:27-29).

Some of the names of Jesus confirm that he was a human – such as 'rabbi' which literally meant 'my great one'. All good Jewish teachers were addressed in this way (John 20:16). Jesus answered to these names, but he also called himself 'I am', which was a name of God so holy that even the Jews dared not say it aloud (Exodus 3:14, John 8:58).

Those who wrote about him in the New Testament used some of the other names for Jesus, which implied that he was not only a man, but God. Matthew called him 'Emmanuel', meaning 'God is with us'. In Jesus, God himself was walking on our planet (Matthew 1:23).

3 ADVERTISING (15 minutes)

Give out photocopies of the poster 'Coming soon' from page 22, one to each subgroup. Ask them to imagine the (impossible, of course) situation that they were advertising an event at which Jesus would be the 'star' speaker. They are to design a poster encouraging people to attend. On it they may write or draw any features of his lifestyle or events from his life that would thrill people enough to leave their armchairs and televisions on a winter evening to go and find out about Jesus. They could include qualities of his character that they admire, or supernatural elements of his life that demand attention. Ask them to talk for several minutes about what they want to include, so that the finished poster is a joint statement from the group. (You could alternatively provide them with paper and felt markers to make a larger presentation.) Allow plenty of time for groups to look at each others' ideas and compare them.

4 TALK (5 minutes)

Mention some of the great features of Jesus' humanity that have emerged from the posters – his compassion, healing, love of peace, sinlessness, and so on. All these would earn Jesus a place in history. One thing makes Jesus different from other great achievers of history – he claimed to be God himself.

Was he insane? He would have to be mad to insist on his divinity to the death if it were not true.

Was he evil? Such a claim would be utterly wicked and blasphemous if it were not true.

Was he speaking the truth? Could Jesus have risen from the dead three days after being executed if his claim to be God were false? The evidence of his lifestyle shown on the posters does not point to a madman, nor is it conceivable that these were the actions of a wicked man. There is only one other possibility. Luke 5:8 shows what happened when Peter worked this out for himself.

5 DISCUSSION (15 minutes)

Lead an open discussion on the question: 'Can you accept that this man Jesus was God?' Start off by inviting someone to disagree with the talk you have just given. Resist the temptation to reply in person, instead asking someone else in the group to offer a different point of view. Continue in this way, inserting some of these quotations at points where the discussion is flagging, needs to take a new turn, or has drifted unhelpfully from the main subject.

GLENN HODDLE
FOOTBALLER AND MANAGER:

"I went to Israel to play for England. We were taken to Bethlehem to see the birthplace of Jesus. Up to that point, for me Jesus was just a story. But when I went and saw where he had lived, I can only say that I had an inner conviction that the story was true. When I went back home I started to read the Bible and talk to some Christians ... I found answers to the questions I was asking ... Jesus came to show us that God really does love us and Christ has given us the chance to find out what life is all about."

C S LEWIS
AUTHOR OF 'THE LION, THE WITCH AND THE WARDROBE':

"You can shut him up for a fool, you can spit at him and kill him as a demon, or you can fall at his feet and call him Lord and God. But let us not come with any patronizing nonsense about his being just a great human teacher. He has not left that open to us. He did not intend to."

DICK FRANCE
THEOLOGIAN AND WRITER:

" Within a few years of Jesus' death and resurrection, his followers had begun to worship him. There could be no clearer evidence that they believed he was God..., a man with whom they had lived not many years before. It was not an easy option, but it was the only way to make sense of what they had seen and heard. "

NAPOLEON BONAPARTE
SOLDIER AND CONQUERING EMPEROR:

" I know men and I tell you, Jesus is more than a man. Comparison is impossible between him and any other human being who ever lived, because he was the Son of God. "

LORD CALDECOTE
FORMER LORD CHIEF JUSTICE OF ENGLAND:

" The gospels and other writings of the men who had been friends of Jesus Christ seem to me to make an overwhelming case merely as a matter of strict evidence, for the facts stated therein. "

FYODOR DOSTOYEVSKY
CLASSIC RUSSIAN WRITER:

" I believe there is no one lovelier, deeper, more sympathetic and more perfect than Jesus ... not only is there no one else like him, but there could never be anyone like him. "

C J CADOUX
PROFESSOR OF HISTORY:

" Jesus invented? The idea is quite fantastic, and has not been championed, so far as I know, by any competent historian. "

CLIFF RICHARD
SINGER:

" During those extraordinary minutes of history, Jesus, who had no sin of his own and could therefore be absolutely at one and in harmony with his Father, took on the sin of the whole of humanity... I'm only grateful, and want my life to be a thank you to the God who now accepts me... because Jesus wiped the slate clean. "

6 *TESTIMONY* (5 minutes)
One of the leaders or a teenager should talk about why and how he or she came to the conclusion that the evidence about Jesus demanded belief, and what difference that made to life. It should definitely include a section about the speaker's present relationship with the ascended Jesus, stressing his role as a living reality, not just a historical character.

7 *PRAYER* (5 minutes)
The leader should say a prayer that if Jesus truly is God and is alive in Heaven, he will make it clear to each individual in the room in a way that puts it beyond doubt.

Invite all present to choose one of the names of Jesus, or one of the meanings, that seems significant to them today. They could choose another phrase if one is not available on the sheet which expresses their viewpoint (if, for example, they have honest doubts). Together, they are to shout out: 'Jesus, you are ...' – the first three words in chorus, the rest in such chaos that only God will identify what is said.

APPROACH 2: *PIONEER*

1 *WHAT DO YOU THINK?* (2minutes)

Give out photocopies of the sheet 'Jesus who?' (page 21), a list of statements about Jesus which have been made by teenagers. Ask the group to tick one box in each line to indicate (to themselves, for it need not be made public) how they accept the historical Jesus.

2 *TALK* (3 minutes)

It is widely accepted that Jesus was a great example of human goodness, courage and kindness. The Christians who wrote the Bible, and today's Christians, held him to be much more than this.

They thought he:

✔ Was perfectly good and loving - the only person to have lived without doing wrong of any kind.

✔ Was God himself, living on this planet in human form.

✔ Rose from the dead miraculously, three days after being executed.

✔ Is alive now in Heaven and is able to listen and help like any other mate.

3 *DISCUSSION* (5 minutes)

Invite any of the group to say whether they find this believable, or just a fairy-tale. Open the question for discussion, being prepared to be put on the spot and explain why you personally have come to accept that Jesus is what he claimed to be. Make sure that the views of those who cannot accept that Jesus was more than a good human, or that he existed at all, have a fair hearing. Close by reading one of the quotations opposite, possibly the one by Napoleon. (2 Corinthians 5:21, Acts 2:22-24,33)

APPROACH 3: *CHALLENGER*

1 *TIME-LINE* (15 minutes)

Split the group into subgroups of four or five. Give each subgroup a pen and a batch of white self-adhesive address labels. Ask them to think of as many different events as they can from the life of Jesus, eg his birth, his baptism, the last supper, etc. They are to write each one on a separate address label.

After several minutes, stretch a clothes-line across the room. The first group should read out one of the events they have recalled, then stick the label on the clothes-line. The second group reads out a different event and adds it to the clothes-line (on the left of the first one if it happened before it; on the right if it happened later). This continues, subsequent groups only suggesting events that have not been mentioned before, until no group has another label to add, and a time-line has been created across the room placing the events of Jesus' life in chronological order. (As long as the principal events are in their logical sequence, there is no need to worry unduly about the precise order.)

2 *TALK* (5 minutes)

Use the talk to focus firstly on any important omissions that are noticeable on the time-line and need to be added.

☐ *Pick out four things that may or may not have been indicated by the groups' contributions:*

☐ *Christ existed eternally, so his birth in Bethlehem should not be the first item on the time-line (Colossians 1:15-17).*

☐ *He is alive now, ascended and glorified in Heaven. His presence at this meeting can be added to the time-line as another episode in the story of Jesus' involvement with our world (Colossians 3:1).*

☐ *He is and was in every way God, glimpsed occasionally in his earthly life (Mark 9:2-7, Colossians 2:9).*

☐ *He was, however, in every way a man, being aware of pain, emotion, sexuality, joy and temptation (Hebrews 4:15).*

3 CURRICULUM VITAE (15 minutes)

Give out photocopies of page 21, explaining what a curriculum vitae is. Suggest that the subgroups each work to complete a CV for Jesus, researching information about the human life and qualities of Christ from the Bible references. When they reach the 'referees' section, they may like to consider how convincing is the evidence on which these eye-witnesses formed their opinions of Jesus.

4 ADMIRATION (10 minutes)

Give each person a file card and ask them to write on it: 'The thing I most admire about Jesus is....'. They should then complete the sentence in a way which is personally true (they may wish to list several things).

When all have finished, collect the cards in, shuffle them and deal them out so that no one gets their own card back. Ask each member of the group to read out the card in his or her hand, leaving a pause after each one so that everyone can reflect on what was said and use it as part of their own worship of Jesus.

5 DISCUSSION (10 minutes)

Read Luke 5:1-11, one person reading the narrative, with two others contributing the voices of Jesus and Simon Peter. Then discuss these questions:

? Why do you think this event made such a deep impression on Simon Peter that he had the reaction described in verse 8?

? Is it true that, because the love and friendship of Jesus is so precious to us, we do not consider the 'dreadful' holiness of Jesus as much as we should?

? What difference would it make if we were more like Peter more of the time?

6 PRAISE (5 minutes)

Use any of the ideas that have emerged about Jesus from this session to honour him in a time of praise to which anyone may contribute a sentence or read a verse from the Bible.

JESUS WHO?

Who do you think Jesus was? Tick one of the boxes to show whether you accept these ways that people have described Jesus.

TICK BOX

YES   NOT SURE   NO

HE LIVED MANY YEARS AGO

HE WAS A GOOD MAN

A SWEAR-WORD

THE BEST TEACHER EVER

HE WAS GOD IN HUMAN FORM

HE COULD WORK MIRACLES

A BIT LIKE A VICAR

HE DIED, BUT CAME ALIVE AGAIN

SOMEONE TO JOKE ABOUT

HE IS ALIVE NOW IN HEAVEN

CURRICULUM VITAE

Summary of my life so far.

Jesus

PERSONAL

Name: (Luke 2:21)

Date of birth: (Matthew 2:1)

Place of birth: (Luke 2:6)

Adult home town: (Matthew 4:13)

Marital status: (assumed)

Education: (Luke 2:46-47, 51-52)

WORKING LIFE

Apprenticeship trade: (Mark 6:3)

Main occupation: (Luke 4:15)

Features of main occupation:
(Matthew 9:35-36; 17:22-23)

REFEREES

First referee: (1 Peter 2:22-23)

Referee's comment about Jesus' qualities

Second referee: (Matthew 7:28-29)

Referee's comment about Jesus' qualities

Third referee: (Matthew 14:25-33)

Referee's comment about Jesus' qualities

Fourth referee: (Mark 1:10-11)

Referee's comment about Jesus' qualities

NOT SO TRIVIAL PURSUIT?

What do these names which the Bible gives to Jesus imply? Guess at one answer for each.

SON OF GOD
1. Uniquely close to God
2. Unhuman
3. Prince of heaven
4. Holy Child

CHRIST
1. Cross bearer
2. Surname
3. Anointed, like a king
4. Message to the world

SON OF MAN
1. Everything best about being a man
2. Human who will reign eternally with God
3. Unable to identify his father
4. One who ignores women

RABBI
1. Worker of miracles
2. God's worker
3. My great teacher
4. Clever as a rabbit

MESSIAH
1. Cross bearer
2. Surname
3. Anointed, like a king
4. Message to the world

JESUS
1. Perfect one
2. God saves us
3. Born in a stable
4. Miracle

EMMANUEL
1. Man of holiness
2. God is with us
3. Eminent among men
4. Instruction book

I AM
1. Unkillable
2. One who brings hope
3. Utterly holy God
4. The way, the truth and the life

COMING SOON TO A CHURCH NEAR YOU!

JESUS CHRIST

LATE NITE XTRA

22

CHAPTER 3

FOLLOWING JESUS

WHAT'S THE BIG IDEA?

This programme reminds teenagers that Jesus has asked for a commitment that goes beyond knowledge that he was a historical character, and beyond casual attendance at a church group to which all their friends go – important though these things are. To those who have grown up in Christian families without considering that there are alternative points of view, it says: 'Be sure you weigh up the cost of following Jesus now.' To those who do not have that kind of background, it says: 'Jesus is worth following, but to follow him requires action.'

PRINCIPAL BIBLE PASSAGE
LUKE 5:27-32

MAJOR POINTS THAT CAN BE MADE

✔ Jesus calls us to action, not just a casual recognition that he exists. He calls us to joy, but not to a life free from hardship, challenge or effort.

OTHER PASSAGES USED
LUKE 9:23-25; 14:27-30, JOHN 10:10;
12:26, ACTS 2:38, ROMANS 10:9-10,
GALATIANS 2:20, JAMES 2:17-20

✔ It is important to be honest with ourselves about where we stand with Jesus – not just avoid the issue in the hope that it is not relevant to our lives.

✔ Unless we weigh up the pros and cons of committing ourselves to Jesus' way, our faith in him may fizzle out when it meets obstacles, and his ability to fulfil us will be impaired.

APPROACH 1: INVESTIGATOR

1 TAKE A WALK (15 minutes)

The leader should invite the group to form pairs. Ask each pair to agree that one of them should be 'leader' and the other 'follower'. When they have decided, announce that all the followers are to be blindfolded. The unsighted one is to follow the other on a trip round the building, possibly even outside it. He or she is to follow the instructions (left, right, forward, etc) that the partner is giving. Make it clear to the leaders that they are not to take their blindfolded companions anywhere unsafe, then send them off on a five minute journey.

Gather the group together and pose some

RESOURCES
'JOURNEY INTO LIFE', NORMAN
WARREN, FALCON
'JOURNEY INTO LIFE: THE VIDEO',
CHURCH PASTORAL AID SOCIETY

questions. In the first place, those taking part should give the answers just to their partners:

A. To those who were blindfolded: What feelings did you have at various stages during the walk?

B. To those who were leaders: What was the most significant moment for you during the walk?

C. To the 'blind': Was your partner a good leader?

D. To leaders: Was your partner a good follower?

After all four questions have been posed, invite them to share with all the rest of the group the highlights of the walk in a more open discussion. Try to draw attention to the fact that following brings both unexpected joys and unexpected problems; that there are good and bad leaders; that there are cooperative and uncooperative followers.

2 WHAT KIND OF A FOLLOWER? (5 minutes)

Give out photocopies of page 28. Explain: 'Everyone follows something! What do you follow?' Invite the group to draw a pinman on each rope in the gym. It should indicate how seriously they are followers of fashion, followers of current affairs, etc. (The climbing pinman need not go at one extreme or the opposite; it could go in the middle or nearer one end than the other.) Use this exercise to lead into the next section.

3 WHERE ARE YOU? (5 minutes)

Ask the group to look at the picture of Jesus striding along a path toward Heaven (photocopied from page 29 and distributed). Ask them to visualise where they might appear on the picture. Are they close beside Jesus? Following him at a distance? Back turned and running defiantly away? Not yet past the cross? They are to draw themselves in the picture, using the symbols of a cross and so on, in any way which seems appropriate. This is a private exercise, so they can be as honest as they like.

4 SKETCH (7 minutes)

With much solemnity, introduce 'Major-General Pugh-Grunting (retired)'. Go out of the room and lead him in. He is wearing thick glasses, and stumbling into objects. Hanging around his shoulders and waist are a rucksack, saucepans, kettles, irons, sledgehammers and a variety of cumbersome equipment. He carries a clipboard. He faces away from the group and starts to address the wall, speaking in the clipped, enthusiastic, public-school voice of a stereotyped adventurer. Someone turns him to face the group and he says, 'Thank you madam' (if it is a man).

Major-General:

"Well, thank you for coming, men. As you know, you are here because you are about to follow me on the first British expedition to conquer the Himalayan Peak K3.

"I must not start without paying tribute to Colonel Gonner, who was to have co-led this expedition with me. As you know, he is unable to join us after the notorious Nepalese incident. He was, you will remember, camped on the freezing slopes within a stone's throw of surmounting Mount Raja, when he slipped out of the tent to answer a call of nature. Now it's cold out there at night, men, I can tell you! We can only sympathise with Colonel Gonner in his delight at finding what he took to be a discarded woolly blanket to wrap around him as he went about his business. We do congratulate him on being the first Britisher to be able to confirm the existence of the legendary bum-biting yeti of Katmandu. And commiserate with him for discovering that the creature is, as we suspected, carnivorous.

Colonel Gonner is now in Bhaktapur Hospital in ward four … and five … and six.

"I'm honoured to take the Colonel's place. Now I must admit, men, I've never been to the Himalayas before. However, I have been up the Whispering Gallery in St Paul's, and pretty scary it was too, I can tell you.

"You can be sure, though, that you are not following a lost cause, because I have taken a trip to Smiths and bought a world map. *(He gets out a large picture of a white man or woman in a swimming costume – either a poster or from a clothes catalogue.)* Now as you know, the pink bits show the extent of the British Empire. *(Peering closely)* Good golly! I didn't realise we still had so much of it. We are setting off from *your town* here, and our destination is obviously this mountainous area here *(he points to appropriate places on the picture).*

"Now, I can assure you, men, that no one is more distressed than I that the supplies we requisitioned from HMG have not materialised.

Fear not, for all is not lost. I have taken the precautionary measure of sending my faithful secretary Dolly down to Liptons. She has purchased ninety packets of Vesta beef curry with rice. These should keep us going for some time – at least until we get to the Everest MacDonalds.

"Now, let's synchronise watches – mine is now reading four minutes past Timex. I'll see you all tomorrow morning by the entrance to platform seven of Victoria Station at ten minutes to 0-eight-hundred hours. Don't be late or you will miss the opportunity to travel by cheap rate blue day pensioner's non-return travel-card holder unaccompanied super-saver. Be sure to go to the right place and don't get mixed up with the rival party which is claiming to offer an adventurous and fulfilling expedition beginning at the King's Cross. I think you men are a shrewd judge of who is good leader. And besides, I've got the compass *(he gets out a pair of compasses).* Follow me, men." *(Exit, through a window, or crashing into a door frame.)*

5 DISCUSSION (20 minutes)

Ask the group to break into subgroups of four or five people. They are to compile two lists; firstly of things they feel are good and positive about following Christ, secondly of things they feel are hard or unexciting about following him.

After a few minutes the subgroups join back into a larger group. Display a chart on which their ideas can be combined, again in two columns. As they call out their suggestions, the leader should write them on the chart, correcting any factual mistakes that may emerge (for example, that being a Christian precisely equals being good and not misbehaving).

When the chart is complete, invite the teenagers to return to subgroups with one frank question to discuss: 'Do the good and positive things outweigh the hard and unexciting things?'

6 TALK (5 minutes)

Use the talk to give your personal view on why the positive values of following Jesus have so outweighed the costs that you have put you faith in him.

Why follow Jesus?

✔ Because he loves and accepts us (Galatians 2:20).

✔ Because he forgives us (Acts 2:38).

✔ Because he fulfils us in a way that fashion, music, politics, horoscopes or anything else we follow never could (John 10:10).

Read Luke 9:23-25 and talk about the challenge and the sacrifice of following Jesus. 'Taking up the cross' implies hardship – it means making every decision on the basis of what Jesus wants, rather than purely selfish motives. But it gives life a joyous purpose that it never had before.

Invite anyone who wants to find out more about what following Jesus means in practice to talk to one of the leaders of the group.

7 PRAYER (3 minutes)

Ask everyone to shut their eyes and imagine themselves to be on the road which they drew themselves on. Jesus is walking ahead of them, and he turns and beckons to them with a warm smile. What will they do? If they want to follow Jesus, ask them to imagine themselves going to him. If they do not, they are to imagine themselves turning away. Or perhaps they stay where they are, still unsure.

The leader should then say a prayer thanking Jesus for his love, forgiveness and offer of fulfilment. Ask him to accept those who have run to him in mind, and never to let them go.

APPROACH 2 : PIONEER

1 STUNT (2 minutes)

Produce a hard-boiled egg. Persuade one of the group to put it down the back of their jeans so that it comes to rest in the place that nature seems to have provided exclusively for the purpose of this exercise. Assure your volunteer that you have hard boiled the egg, and ask him or her three questions:

? Does he or she believe you?

? Does he or she trust that you would not play a mean trick?

? Is he or she prepared to act on this belief and trust by sitting down on a hard chair?

2 TALK (3 minutes)

Pose the question: 'What does it mean to follow Jesus?' The three points of the answer are related to the three questions of the stunt:

A. It means believing in the facts about his life, death and resurrection. But not just that!

B. It means trusting that Jesus is able to give a more fulfilled life to those who let him take control of their lives. But not just that!

C. It means acting on what you believe, deciding to start a relationship with him and changing to fit his plans.

(Luke 5:27-28, Romans 10:9-10, James 2:17-20)

3 DISCUSSION (4 minutes)

Ask the group members to consider how far they have got along that three-stage process – do they believe the facts, or trust that Jesus can make a difference, or have they decided to be one of his followers? Or are they not even at the first stage? Ask whether anyone is prepared to tell the others where they stand. Invite the rest to comment on what they think of that person's decision, but stress that they are not to be insulting in their reply. If no one wants to comment, the leader should tell them where he or she stands.

4 CHALLENGE (1 minute)

Close with a brief challenge to go beyond the facts and try out the possibility of making Jesus a part of life. 'Start by talking to him about something that really matters to you (praying), and see what happens...'

APPROACH 3: CHALLENGER

1 WHERE ARE YOU? (5 minutes)

Ask the group to look at the picture of Jesus striding along a path toward Heaven (photocopied from page 29 and distributed). Ask them to visualise where they might appear on the picture. Are they close beside Jesus? Following him at a distance? Back turned and running defiantly away? Not yet past the cross? They are to draw themselves in the picture, using the symbols of a cross and so on, in any way which seems appropriate.

This is a private exercise, so they can be as honest as they like.

2 BIBLE STUDY (10 minutes)

Read Luke 5:27-32 and explain the position of a tax collector in Jesus' time, despised by the Jews because they worked for the occupying Romans and extorted more than they were entitled to so as to line their own pockets. Levi, who is elsewhere known as Matthew, was later to become one of the apostles.

Split the group into fours and invite them to answer these questions as if they were Levi. They are printed under 'Answer this!' on page 28, which could be photocopied for convenience. The answers should be written down.

1 Levi, how did the process of following Jesus begin for you?

2 How would you describe your life before you encountered Jesus?

3 When Jesus called you to follow him, what did you think it meant, Levi?

4 Did following Jesus mean an instant transformation or a slow process of discovery?

5 Levi, how has following Jesus changed your life?

3 CHAT SHOW (5 minutes)

The leader should invite one pair to come to the front of the room and act out the questions and answers they have devised as if they were giving an interview on a chat show. Familiar theme music and applause could be used for added impact!

4 MY STORY (10 minutes)

The leader should explain that (s)he will give the group the five questions again. This time, however, they are to work individually and answer the questions as if they were addressed to them personally, and were about their own experience of following Christ. They will probably get most out of this if they write down their answers again.

5 SHARING THE STORY (10 minutes)

The groups go back into fours. They are to tell the others in this subgroup the answers, each person 'interviewing' the person on his or her left, in the style of the chat show given earlier. Since each person only has two minutes to give their answers, tell the groups not to let any one person talk endlessly.

6 BIBLE GAME (10 minutes)

Split the group into relay teams, ask them to remove their watches and cover the clocks. Explain that the race will take place with a strict time limit, say three minutes. At the far end of the room, place a big pile of toy building bricks. The teams are to run one at a time to the pile and pick up one brick each. They return to their team with it, but they may not start to build yet. The next member of the team then runs to collect a brick and so on. At any point the team may collectively decide to stop collecting and start building a tower with the bricks they have obtained. After that point they may not go back for any more bricks. When the time is up, a whistle blows and the teams must stop building, whether or not their tower is finished. The highest tower wins.

Allow the teams time to talk about tactics before they begin. They must be careful not to spend so much time collecting bricks that they are unable to build them before the whistle blows. On they other hand, they should try to obtain an optimum number of bricks so that they are not left with wasted time at the end.

Play the game twice so that they can learn from their mistakes on the second run.

7 TALK (5 minutes)

Read Luke 14:27-30. Point out that the teams have just played out this parable as a game. Make these points:

✔ *There is a cost to following Jesus: 'Carrying your own cross'. It means different things to different people – unpopularity, hardship, forsaking ambitions, doing without possessions. It will not mean all of these, but it will certainly involve some.*

✔ *You need to weigh the cost of following Jesus every time you set out on a new stage of your relationship with him. He has warned us of this so that our good intentions do not come to nothing.*

✔ *We 'carry the cross' not because God wants to make things difficult for us, but because he sees it as the best way for us to find fulfilment in him. The joy of it is having Jesus with us now and forever, and having God honour us (John 12:26). Let that sink in – God will honour us!*

8 PRAYER (5 minutes)

Return to the sheet 'Answer this!', taken from page 28. In the lower sections of the cross, individuals are to write two things. Firstly, they finish the sentence; 'Because I follow Jesus....' in a way which is personally true to them. It could express the joy of his friendship, the assurance of his presence through eternity, or something new they have learnt recently.

They are then to consider what they currently find most challenging or daunting about following Christ and use it to complete the sentence: 'The cross that I need help to carry is ...'. After a couple of minutes working alone with God to write these sentences, invite them to use these thoughts in a time of open prayer.

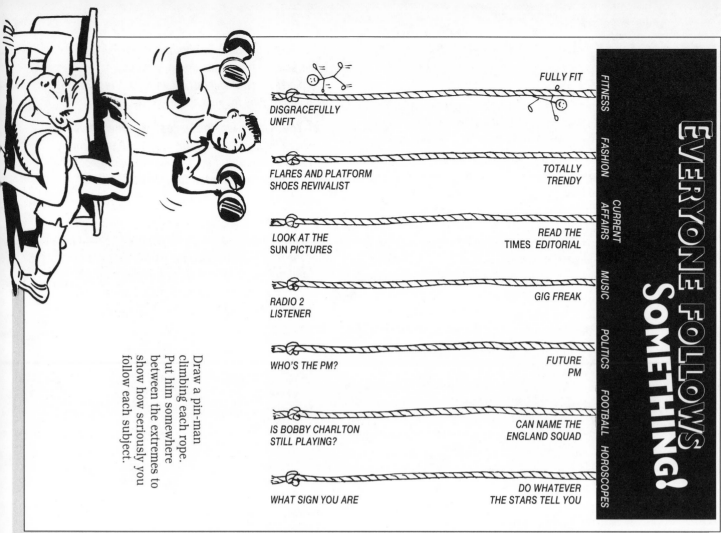

EVERYONE FOLLOWS SOMETHING!

FITNESS	FULLY FIT	DISGRACEFULLY UNFIT
FASHION	TOTALLY TRENDY	FLARES AND PLATFORM SHOES REVIVALIST
CURRENT AFFAIRS	READ THE TIMES EDITORIAL	LOOK AT THE SUN PICTURES
MUSIC	GIG FREAK	RADIO 2 LISTENER
POLITICS	FUTURE PM	WHO'S THE PM?
FOOTBALL	CAN NAME THE ENGLAND SQUAD	IS BOBBY CHARLTON STILL PLAYING?
HOROSCOPES	DO WHATEVER THE STARS TELL YOU	WHAT SIGN YOU ARE

Draw a pin-man climbing each rope. Put him somewhere between the extremes to show how seriously you follow each subject.

ANSWER THIS!

HOW WOULD YOU DESCRIBE YOUR LIFE BEFORE YOU ENCOUNTERED JESUS?

HOW DID YOU COME TO START FOLLOWING JESUS?

WHEN JESUS CALLED YOU TO FOLLOW HIM, WHAT DID YOU THINK IT MEANT?

DID FOLLOWING JESUS MEAN AN INSTANT TRANSFORMATION OR A SLOW PROCESS OF DISCOVERY?

HOW HAS FOLLOWING JESUS CHANGED YOUR LIFE?

BECAUSE I FOLLOW JESUS...

THE 'CROSS' THAT I NEED HELP TO CARRY IS...

28

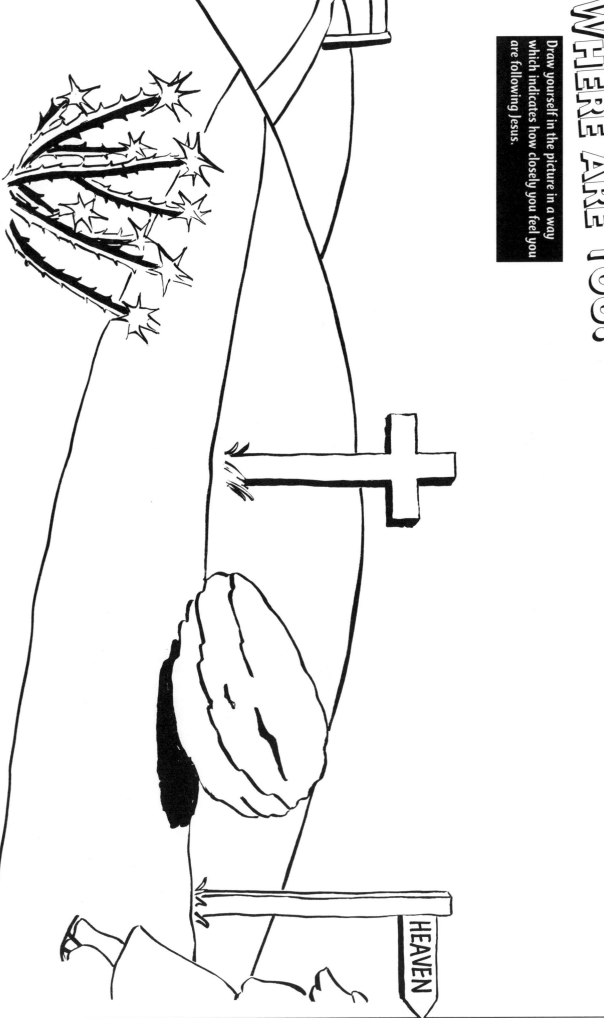

CHAPTER 4

WHAT DOES GOD WANT TO DO FOR ME?

WHAT'S THE BIG IDEA?

The Holy Spirit is explored in this programme as God's means of doing exciting things in a person's life. In different ways, teenagers are asked to identify in themselves areas in which they feel they could be better people, and to open themselves to the Holy Spirit filling them and growing his 'fruit' in that area.

Items from Approaches 1 and 3 can always be substituted for each other, but more so than most with this programme.

PRINCIPAL BIBLE PASSAGE
2 TIMOTHY 1:6-7

MAJOR POINTS THAT CAN BE MADE

◆ God lives on earth in spirit form; in a sense he dwells 'inside' Christians. He can either stay in a little religious corner of our lives, or fill every part of us with the things God plans for us.

◆ The qualities the Holy Spirit wants to bring out are tough and appealing ones, such as power, love, self-control.

◆ He offers us help as we pray, as we learn about God, as we seek to behave in a godly way, as we try to work on God's behalf.

◆ Two metaphors help – the 'fruit' of the Spirit brings out good flavours in us, the 'flame' of the Spirit burns away rubbish and brings light to parts of our lives which would otherwise be in darkness.

OTHER PASSAGES USED
JOHN 14:15-27; 16:7-10,13-15,
ACTS 1:8; 2:1-4, ROMANS 8:9,15,26-27,
1 CORINTHIANS 12:1-11, 2 CORINTHIANS
3:18, GALATIANS 5:16-23, EPHESIANS
3:16-19, 1 THESSALONIANS 5:19,
1 PETER 1:7-8, 1 JOHN 1:5-7

APPROACH 1: INVESTIGATOR

1 GAME (5 minutes)
Divide the young people into two groups. Draw a line across the floor and stand one group on each side of the line. Declare that the playing area extends one metre on either side of the line and that no one must step out of the area. The idea is to reach out, grab members of the opposing team, and pull them across the line. As soon as a player has both feet across the line, he must change teams and try to pull his former team-members across. After a given time, the people who are at that moment in the larger team are declared the winners.

RESOURCES
'THE HOLY SPIRIT', CLIVE CALVER,
SCRIPTURE UNION
'COME HOLY SPIRIT', DAVID PYTCHES,
HODDER AND STOUGHTON

2 BIBLE STUDY (10 minutes)
State that God is longing to give good things to those who belong to him. As in the game, it is only our own resistance which can stop him working within us to bring about what he knows is best for our lives.

Give out photocopies of the sheet 'Opposites' from page 35, and split those present into subgroups of four or five. Explain that the sentences on the left hand side were written in a letter by Paul to a church about thirty years after Jesus died. Ask the subgroups to work together to come up with sentences which convey the complete opposite, then write them in the appropriate boxes. Suggest that humour might not be out of place as they work out the awful extremes.

3 REFLECTION (5 minutes)

Ask each person, working now as an individual, to decide where their current state of mind appears to fit between the two extremes. They circle one of the pinmen to indicate where they feel they belong.

4 TALK (5 minutes)

Make these points:

♦ God wants to change our lifestyle to the attractive features in the left-hand column. This kind of transformation is impossible without help – even for Christians. For this reason, God has given us a helper – the Holy Spirit. This is God living on earth, as it were 'inside' people, in spirit form (John 14:15-17).

♦ These are a few of the innumerable ways in which he helps us:

✔ Praying for us and taking our prayers to God (Romans 8:26-27).

✔ Reminding us what God wants us to do (John 16:13-15).

✔ Making us powerful and loving (2 Timothy 1:7).

✔ Equipping us to work for the good of the world and the service of God (1 Corinthians 12:1-11).

♦ The Spirit is with every believer, *but* it is up to us how much we open ourselves to him. He either stays in a little religious corner of our lives or, if we consciously want and ask him to, he *fills* every part of us with the things God plans for us (Ephesians 3:16-19).

5 GROWING LIKE JESUS (20 minutes)

Explain that in one of his letters Paul describes what God wants to do for people as a growing fruit. Read Galatians 5:22-23 to show what the Holy Spirit can and will produce in people if he is allowed to.

Give out photocopies of the sheet 'Growing like Jesus' from page 36. Split the group into subgroups and give each subgroup a few sheets of brightly coloured paper, pairs of scissors and felt-tipped pens. On the wall, display a big picture of a bare tree. (The illustration on page 36 should help you.)

Ask each subgroup to cut nine fruit shapes from the coloured paper. They should divide up the work between them (the shapes on the photocopied sheets may help). When this is completed, they should write the nine 'flavours' of the fruit of the Holy Spirit on them, one on each. Share out the fruit shapes so that each of the subgroup has two or three. They are to look at the quality described on the front, then think of one situation when we all might need the power of the Holy Spirit to bring this out in us. For instance, for 'Faithfulness' someone might write: 'I need my friends to stick by me when I'm having parent-trouble, and I need to keep secrets that have been trusted to me.' When they have done this, they are to share with the rest of the subgroup what they have written.

Regain everyone's attention to tell them that God is ready to bring out all these features in people; indeed he longs to. It is up to us to hand ourselves over to the Holy Spirit to be filled by him, consciously asking him to take control. Provide Blu-Tack and ask everyone to fix the fruits they have made to the tree on the wall.

6 AFFIRMATION AND PRAYER (15 minutes)

Ask each person to cut out a number of fruits from the 'Growing like Jesus' sheet. They should cut out the same number of fruits as there are people in their subgroup.

They are to consider each person in their subgroup and decide which of the nine features they feel is most strongly evident in that person's life. This might be the measured observation of a lifetime's friendship, or a gut feeling based on meeting for the first time this session. On one of the fruits they write the name of the person and the feature they have chosen. Everybody writes one for himself or herself too.

This complete, the leader should set the tone for a sincere sharing of affirmation in each subgroup. One person in each subgroup stays silent, while the rest of them take turns to give him or her the fruit that bears his or her name and explain why they chose the feature that they most appreciate. The person who has received the cut-out fruits should then say which feature he chose for himself. Repeat this process for each person in the subgroup.

Close with a few moments of silent prayer in which each teenager is asked to thank God for the person sitting on his or her left.

APPROACH 2: PIONEER

1 OPINIONS (3 minutes)

On four large sheets of card, draw the outlines of four faces (the pictures on page 36 may help you). They should have eyes, ears and mouths, but completely bald heads. Each character has a name and an adjective printed beneath it:

- ●◆ WIMPY WILLY: timid
- ●◆ MIGHTY MADGE: powerful
- ●◆ KIND KEVIN: loving
- ●◆ COOL KELLY: self-controlled

Give each member of the group a felt marker. They are to decide how important they think those characteristics are in a human being, rating them between one and five points. After a moment to think, they all have a chance to put hairs on the heads - one hair if they think it is an unimportant characteristic, five if they think it is very important. (Double the hairs if it is a small group.) When this has been done, compare hairiness to discover the group's collective opinion.

2 TALK (3 minutes)
Make these points:

♦ *Jesus promised to make our lives great, in no sense an oppressive matter of obeying rules. His greatest gift to us is the Holy Spirit, God himself 'living inside' Christians.*

♦ *What does the Holy Spirit do for us? Read 2 Timothy 1:7 as one example. He gives us:*

✔ *POWER – because the Spirit within us gives us a direct link to God, the greatest power-source of all, when we pray.*

✔ *LOVE – because the Spirit changes the way we appreciate each other; reassuring us that God loves us, allowing us to enjoy each other in a more fulfilling way.*

✔ *Self-control – because Jesus asks a lot of us in obedience and commitment, and we need the Spirit's help to stop us failing him time and time again.*

You can't seriously prefer a life of timidity! (Romans 8:9, 2 Timothy 1:7)

3 DISCUSSION (4 minutes)
Open the subject for a brief discussion. Some questions you might ask the group are: In your experience, do Christians act as though they have power, love and self-control? What difference could it make to have God actually within you? Does what God has to offer through the Holy Spirit sound appealing – why or why not?

APPROACH 3: CHALLENGER

1 BIBLE READING (5 minutes)
Someone should read first John 14:15-27, then Acts 2:1-4. At the climax of the reading, when the Spirit is given, put a candle on a table where all can see it, then light it. Have a time of silence during which everyone watches the candle and considers what God might have wanted to teach us by making a flame the symbol of the Holy Spirit.

2 TALK (3 minutes)
Make these points:

▢ *After Pentecost the Holy Spirit, God himself living within us, continued to be symbolised by a flame. As Christians, the Holy Spirit is within us as our privilege and right. But it is up to us how effective his work is. Paul writes that we can fan this flame so that it burns brighter (2 Timothy 1:6, NIV) or quench it by having contempt for the* work the Holy Spirit does (1 Thessalonians 5:19).

☐ *Why a flame?*

✔ *IT SUGGESTS LIGHT – the Holy Spirit's function is to scatter darkness brought into our lives by sinfulness and bad relationships (1 John 1:5-7).*

✔ *IT SUGGESTS BURNING – getting rid of the rubbish which stops us enjoying God to the full (Galatians 5:16-23).*

✔ *IT SUGGEST REFINING — fire purifies metal, and the Spirit purifies our faith, bringing us joy and love, and bringing Jesus glory and honour (1 Peter 1:7-8).*

To let God do these things for us, we need the continuous process of being filled with the Holy Spirit, consciously allowing him to take control of what is going on in our lives.

③ THE SPIRIT'S HELP (45 minutes)
Give everyone some self-adhesive stickers – the kind which are removable (eg Post-it notes). They are to cut or tear them so that they have eight slips, each with an adhesive part. Give out photocopies of the sheet 'Open to receive' from page 35.

The leader should ask eight searching questions, which everyone should answer as honestly as they can, in the knowledge that no one else will see what they wrote. Each time, they should write the letter of the question and their answer on a sticker and place it on the open hands of the sheet. If they cannot think of an answer, they just write its letter and stick it down on the hands.

The questions are:

A. Of what are you most afraid right now?

B. About what area of life do you find it most difficult to know what is right and what is wrong?

C. What do you find most difficult to understand about God?

D. In what way do you find it hardest to serve God?

E. What do you pray about without seeming to get an answer?

F. What do you do that you know Jesus would never have done?

G. Where, when or with whom do you find it most difficult to show that you are a Christian?

H. What habit do you want to be rid of?

Ask those present to gather into groups of four or five. Display a list of references, written in a vertical column down the left hand side of a sheet of paper, thus:

ROMANS 8:15

JOHN 16:7-10

JOHN 14:26

1 CORINTHIANS 12:4-7

ROMANS 8:27

2 CORINTHIANS 3:18

ACTS 1:8

ROMANS 8:26

Ask the groups to look up each one in turn and, between them, devise one sentence which sums up what it says about what God wants to give us through the Holy Spirit.

When they have done this, go through them, finding out what the groups discovered. Sum them up by writing next to the references, respectively:

DRIVES OUT FEAR

SHOWS US RIGHT FROM WRONG

TEACHES US ABOUT GOD

HELPS US SERVE GOD

PRAYS WITH US

MAKES US LIKE JESUS

GIVES POWER

GIVES STRENGTH

For each of the statements listed on page 34, invite the teenagers to give a score from 0 to 5. 0 means 'this is not true at all'; 5 means 'this sums me up completely'. They are to write the score in the grid beneath the hands, making sure that they put the score in the box number appropriate to the statement.

When this is finished, they add up their scores horizontally and put a total in one of the boxes on the right. Ask them to put the letters A to H in the other right-hand boxes: A at the top to H at the bottom. While they are doing this, the leader should write the same letters against the list of references which was displayed earlier, again A at the top to H at the bottom.

The next few minutes should be treated with some seriousness. Ask them as individuals to decide which letters, A to H, scored highly (they may define for themselves what a high score is, remembering that 20 is the maximum). Explain that the references on the wall show, letter for letter, what help God wants to give them in the high-scoring areas through the Holy Spirit. They should look up those verses again, applying them particularly to the labels on the pair of hands, which have corresponding letters.

Having chosen certain high-scoring areas, suggest that they peel the label off the pair of hands and write in its place a phrase or sentence from the appropriate Bible passage. They put the labels they are symbolically throwing away into a metal bowl or basket. The leader should then take the candle that has been burning throughout the session, remind the group of the Spirit's role in burning away rubbish and bringing light, and set fire to the labels. As they burn, invite the group silently to open themselves to the Holy Spirit doing this in reality to these areas of their lives.

4 PRAYER (5 minutes)

Following the silent prayer, have a time of open prayer in which anyone may thank God for all the things the Holy Spirit does for us, and praying for him to fill the group, bringing with him the gifts that he wants us to use to serve each other.

1 Sometimes I wonder whether or not it is right to do something I want to do.
2 I am not even slightly like Jesus.
3 I want to help others in this group.
4 I'm confused as to how far it is OK to go sexually.
5 I'm scared of dying.
6 People persuade me to do things I don't want to do.
7 I don't know whether God hears me when I pray.
8 When my friends ask me about Jesus, I never know what to say.
9 It seems to me that nothing is completely wrong or completely right – there are grey areas in between.
10 God is so incredible I will never understand him.
11 I get very nervous before big events.
12 Nothing I do for God seems to go right.
13 I wouldn't honestly call myself confident.
14 I wish I was as loving as Jesus was.
15 God does not seem like a loving father to me.
16 God hasn't made me talented at anything much.
17 Stupid little things scare me even though I know they can't harm me.
18 I don't know what to say when it comes to praying.
19 I want to find out more about God.
20 At school/work I keep quiet about being a Christian.
21 My memory of what the Bible says is shocking.
22 I wish Jesus was still here to tell us what is right and what is wrong.
23 I don't know if I pray for the right things.
24 I've never prayed for a miracle.
25 I wish my church would ask me to do more responsible things for the fellowship.
26 When I think about the goodness of Jesus, I feel inadequate.
27 I've got a habit I want to kick, but can't.
28 I don't really understand much of what people say about God.
29 My prayers seem feeble compared with the vast needs of the world.
30 I want people to see that Jesus makes a difference to my life more than they do at present.
31 I keep making resolutions to change my ways, then break them.
32 I am not good enough to meet Jesus face to face.

OPPOSITES

In the empty boxes, write what the Bible might say to give the exact opposite impression.

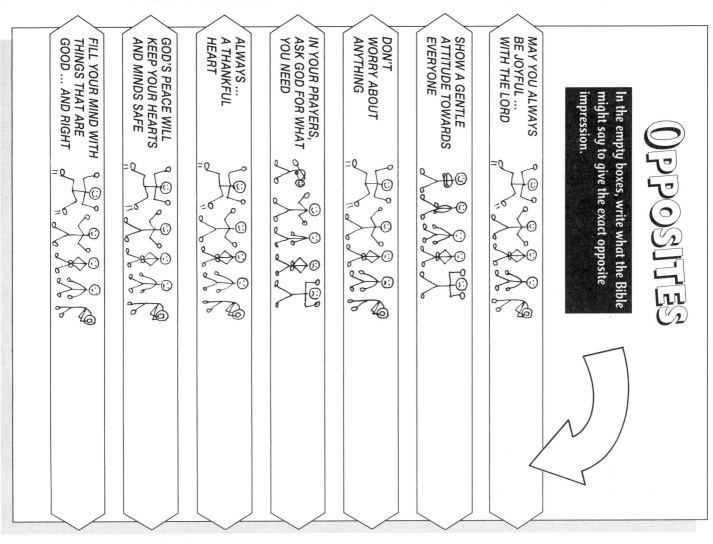

- MAY YOU ALWAYS BE JOYFUL ... WITH THE LORD
- SHOW A GENTLE ATTITUDE TOWARDS EVERYONE
- DON'T WORRY ABOUT ANYTHING
- IN YOUR PRAYERS, ASK GOD FOR WHAT YOU NEED
- ALWAYS ... A THANKFUL HEART
- GOD'S PEACE WILL KEEP YOUR HEARTS AND MINDS SAFE
- FILL YOUR MIND WITH THINGS THAT ARE GOOD ... AND RIGHT

OPEN TO RECEIVE

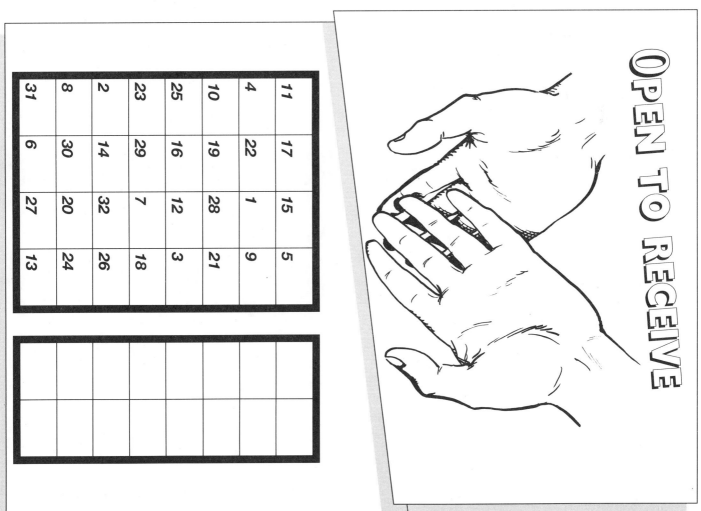

GROWING LIKE JESUS

PEACE

FAITHFULNESS

KINDNESS

JOY

PATIENCE

HUMILITY

LOVE

SELF-CONTROL

GOODNESS

WIMPY WILLY

MIGHTY MADGE

KIND KEVIN

COOL KELLY

CHAPTER 5

HIDDEN INFLUENCES

WHAT'S THE BIG IDEA?

Pop songs flow over teenagers. Their world is full of images of up-to-the-minute fashion, materialist advertising, magazines with maximum style and minimum content. During this session they are encouraged to ask whether there is more to this than meets the eye. Are they in control of the way their minds are shaped, or are they being influenced – even by their peers – in ways of which they are unaware?

PRINCIPAL BIBLE PASSAGE
COLOSSIANS 2:20 - 3:4

MAJOR POINTS THAT CAN BE MADE

✔ Your mind is precious, and people are after it because there is big money to be made from a captured mind!

OTHER PASSAGES USED:
DEUTERONOMY 18:9-11, 1 SAMUEL 16:7, NEHEMIAH 5:15, PSALM 25:4-10; 86:11-12, PROVERBS 3:6-7; 20:14; 23:22-23; 30:18, MATTHEW 6:28-33; 24:4,10-14, LUKE 16:13-15, JOHN 8:31-32; 14:6; 18:38, ROMANS 12:2, GALATIANS 3:27-28, PHILIPPIANS 4:7, 1 TIMOTHY 4:8

✔ Jesus Christ claimed to be 'the Truth'. He set the standard by which influences can be measured. Against him, ways of life which are effectively 'lies', such as materialism, are shown for what they are.

✔ The Holy Spirit is given to 'guard our hearts and minds'. We are instructed to 'set our minds on things in heaven'.

✔ Don't be so taken up with fashion, possessions, street cred and the values of those around you that 'your love goes cold' – either for each other or for God.

APPROACH 1: INVESTIGATOR

1 GAME (15 minutes)

Invite four people to play a role-playing game with you. Send one outside the room and give the other three a role to play. Call the fourth back and sit them on chairs facing inwards. Give them a subject to discuss and ask them to talk about it for approximately three minutes. The first person to speak must be the one who went out of the room, but after that conversation may be ad libbed in any way. After the time is up or the conversation comes to a natural close, ask the fourth person to guess what roles the others were playing. (If the conversation flags, the leader should ask subsidiary questions to keep the chat going.) Three rounds of this game are suggested. Invite different participants each time.

RESOURCES
'FILMS IN CLOSE-UP', ALAN MACDONALD, FRAMEWORKS

ROUND 1

PERSON A: Is mad about money and possessions and shows off his wealth to everyone.

PERSON B: Agrees with what everyone else says, even when it doesn't make sense to do so.

PERSON C: Thinks Britain is great and any other nationality is rubbish.

Question: What kind of holiday would be good for the four of you to go on, and where?

ROUND 2

PERSON A: Male chauvinist pig with no sensitivity to a girl's feelings.

PERSON B: Isn't interested in the conversation and wants to change the subject.

PERSON C: Tries to live by the Bible's standards.

Question: How far should you go on the first date?

ROUND 3

PERSON A: Hates to stand out in a crowd.

PERSON B: Is an up-to-the-minute trendy in all matters of fashion and style.

PERSON C: Likes to shock people.

Question: Have you got any good ideas for what to wear to X's fancy dress party?

2 WHAT INFLUENCES YOU? (10 minutes)

Label the four corners of the room: A lot, quite a lot, a little, not at all. The participants stand in the centre of the room. Call out ten things by which some people are influenced, and ask those present to decide whether they personally are influenced by these things. They are to run to the appropriate corner. Threaten a forfeit or a custard pie in the face of anyone who takes more than ten seconds to decide! The ten influences are:

- ✖ *Up-to-date fashions and styles of clothes.*
- ✖ *Advertisements.*
- ✖ *What the papers say about events.*
- ✖ *What the rest of your friends do and say.*
- ✖ *What nationality or race people are.*
- ✖ *Horoscopes.*
- ✖ *What the Bible teaches us to do.*
- ✖ *Personal likes and dislikes.*
- ✖ *What your parents do and say.*
- ✖ *What appears to give you street cred.*

3 TALK (5 minutes)

Comment on the way the votes split, then make these points:

We are all influenced by something and it is incredibly hard to hold a different opinion from everyone else you know. (The voting probably revealed this.)

It is important to know what influences us, because people are after our minds, and there are hidden influences at work. For example, if you see immoral sexual behaviour accepted as normal on the television again and again, it becomes easy to assume that everyone ought to be doing the same, whether or not God has a different view.

The Bible says: 'Don't let the world around you squeeze you into its mould, but let God remould your minds from within, so that you may prove in practice that the plan of God for you is good' (Romans 12:2, J B Phillips).

Christians say that God's plan for us is good. We must be aware, though, that people whose intentions for us seem neutral can actually have plans which are not all they seem. For instance, be aware that:

✔ Advertisers may be trying to sell you something you don't want.

✔ Fashion changes every year because manufacturers are after your money.

✔ Anyone who stops you in the street to talk about life is biassed (and that includes Christians!).

✔ Newspapers and TV can tell the same story in different ways depending on which person they sympathise with.

✔ You don't *have* to do what everyone else in your age group is doing.

One of the 80's half dozen biggest hits was by a famous-for-fifteen-minutes band called 'Frankie goes to Hollywood'. They say: 'We're living in an age where sex and horror are the new gods.' At least they were honest about what they thought, not using sexuality and materialism in a hidden way. But there was nothing 'hidden' about Jesus, the God of Christians. He said that if we obey him and are his disciples (followers), 'you will know the truth and the truth will set you free' (John 8:31-32). Free to be the best that humans can be! Not a bad offer to consider!

4 POSTERS (15 minutes)

Split the group into subgroups of about six. Invite each subgroup to make two advertising posters. The idea of the posters is to encourage people to buy and read the Bible. The first poster must have no hidden influences, but must present good reasons for finding out the Bible's message in a straightforward, truthful way. The second may use any underhand or hidden method to persuade people that the Bible is worth their attention: half-truths, 'free' gifts, pandering to people's interest in money, suffering or sex, and so on. After discussing what the differences would be, the subgroup may divide up the work on the two posters in any way. Provide paper and felt-tipped pens.

Display the posters when they are complete and comment on the differences. Remind those present how easy it is for advertisers to persuade us to do what they want. Even religions of all kinds can be 'sold' to us in an underhand way. However, Jesus claimed to be 'the Truth' (John 14:6). Ignore the packaging – find out about Jesus himself and make your own opinion about him. If you find yourself agreeing with what he says, then ally yourself with him, and measure all other influences against him.

5 BIBLE DISCUSSION (10 minutes)

Read out a series of Bible verses from the *Good News Bible*, explaining that they are relevant to some of the influences which have been discussed. After each one ask the subgroups to discuss, on the basis of the verse, whether God wants this factor to influence us a lot, quite a lot, a little or not at all. In other words, which corner would *he* have run to? Explain that they are to decide for themselves – they will not be asked to divulge their conclusions:

- FASHION – Matthew 6:28-33
- WHAT EVERYONE ELSE OF MY AGE DOES – Nehemiah 5:15b
- HOROSCOPES – Deuteronomy 18:9-11
- NATIONALITY AND GENDER – Galatians 3:27-28
- SPORT – 1 Timothy 4:8
- ADVERTISING AND PRESSURE TO BUY – Proverbs 20:14
- WHAT YOUR PARENTS SAY – Proverbs 23:22-23
- WHAT GOD WANTS – Proverbs 3:6-7
- STREET CRED – 1 Samuel 16:7
- MATERIALISM – Luke 16:13-15
- ROMANCE – Proverbs 30:18 (deliberately more open-ended)

6 PRAYER (5 minutes)

Read Psalm 25:4-10, with an invitation to those present to make it their own prayer. Ask them to think of one influence on them which they would like to change the impact of. It could be something they want to influence them a lot more (or quite a lot, or a little), or something which currently has a hold on them which they would prefer not to influence them. Thinking of this feature, they should turn on their seats to face the corner which represents what they want to happen to it in future (or go and stand in that space). The leader should say a prayer that God will help them fulfil this. Pray that we may all get the best out of fashion, advertising and the example of the groups we enjoy mixing with, and know when it's right to stand out against them. Close by reading Psalm 86:11-12.

APPROACH 2: PIONEER

1 ADVERTISING SKETCHES (3 minutes)

A group of four people should rehearse and present these spoof TV advertisements. They should be *very* fast moving, lasting only half a minute each. As you introduce them, ask the group to look for 'hidden' messages in them.

1 Luscious music plays. A woman sits in front of a mirror with two tubs beside her. She dips her hand into one and rubs into her left cheek. Then she does the same with the other tub and her right cheek. She looks carefully in the mirror, then declares: 'I can't tell the difference.' A voice-over croons: 'Yes! Statistics prove it. Nine out of every ten women can't tell the difference between margarine and butter.'

2 Four people line up facing the front. The first strikes a cool pose and is wearing trendy clothes. A voice-over says, 'This woman's got one.' The second, a male, is equally trendy and grins. The voice-over says, 'This man's got two.' The third strikes a pose as the voice-over speaks: 'This woman's got an extra long one.' The fourth wears glasses and is thin and spotty. The voice-over declares, 'This man hasn't got one at all.' At this point the first three swing round and reveal long, hanging, furry (or plaited) tassels, hanging like tails from the belts of their jeans. The voice-over says, 'They've all got dingly doobers, the coolest new fashion accessory since ear-muffs.' The fourth man turns round. There is a notice on his bottom saying: 'Too weedy to wear one'.

The voice-over booms, 'Dingly doobers. No dude is dressed without one!'

3 A man stands in the centre. The voice-over intones: 'Persy'. Girls scream, rush in, pull off his sweater and run off. The man regains his composure. The whole process is repeated twice, with the girls ripping off his shirt and T-shirt. They reappear with a bowl full of wet clothes and a box of washing powder. They make rhapsodic noises as they wash the clothes. One says: 'What is this new washing powder, Sharon? It drives me wild when I use it.' The voice-over says: 'Persy. Women can't wait to get their hands on it.'

4 Three people hold pots of mustard. A voice-over speaks: 'What mustard will you put on the side of your plate today?' The person with German mustard steps forward. 'You could choose German mustard. From the country that brought you German measles, the Gestapo, and the First World War. German mustard!' The person with Dutch mustard does the same. 'You could choose Dutch mustard. From the country that brought you Dutch elm disease and double Dutch. If this is mustard I'm a Dutchman.' The person with British mustard swells and the others kneel. They begin to hum *Land of Hope and Glory* and eventually wave Union Jacks. The voice crescendoes. 'But there *is* a mustard which takes all in its stride. Grown in the lush fields of Norfolk, harvested by farmers who have worked the land for generations, processed in historic London where the kings and queens of countless years have graced the throne. This is the mustard of our nation; this is the mustard that rules the world; this is *our* mustard. British mustard!'

2 TALK (3 minutes)
Make these points:

☐ *People are after your mind! Jesus said it would be so. Even advertisements are not always selling you what you think they are.*

☐ *The first one we saw tried to persuade you that margarine can make you beautiful. The statistics are trying to persuade you: 'Everyone else does it, so you must do it too.'*

☐ *The second one tries to persuade you that you absolutely must wear whatever is in fashion. If you think the example is ridiculous, just think how easily teenagers in the seventies were persuaded to wear flares and how, one summer*

in the eighties, girls thought it the height of fashion to wear antennae with furry blobs on called 'Deely-boppers'. It is no accident – it is because someone is making big, big bucks out of it. And incidentally, who says that if you wear glasses and have spots you are a wimp?

☐ *The third one appealed to your sexuality to sell you something that is nothing whatever to do with sex. Very common!*

☐ *The fourth one persuades you that British is good and everything else is rubbish. The ad does not mention taste once! Exaggerated perhaps, until you remember what holiday makers and football supporters say when they are abroad.*

☐ *We have, as a society, made ourselves new gods: the need to be in fashion, the importance of money, the urgency of having an active sex life, boys having to be macho and girls having to be alluring. Neither fashion, nor money, nor sex are bad, but they can be used badly. And people will use them to take advantage of you in hidden ways.*

☐ *Jesus foresaw a time when 'such will be the spread of evil that many people's love will grow cold.' He seemed to have his head screwed on straight in seeing the danger of love being squeezed out. Don't let love for him and love for people get frozen out by hidden influences.*

(Matthew 24:4,10-14)

3 YOUR OPINION (3 minutes)
Ask everyone to stand in the middle of the room. You are going to make some statements. If people agree totally, they stand on the right side of the room. If they disagree, they move to the left side. If they are completely undecided, they stand in the centre, but they may position themselves anywhere else in between if they veer slightly more to one opinion than the other. Do not give the impression that there is a 'correct' answer:

✔ It is vital to have a car to drive once you are seventeen.

✔ If hot pants, flares, plus fours or bondage trousers come back into fashion, I would wear them, even if I don't know what they are!

✔ Advertisements influence what I buy.

✔ It is sophisticated to smoke cigarettes.

✔ Jesus' teaching is relevant to this generation.

✔ Newspapers give you good advice about politics.

✔ Men should earn money; women should look after babies.

✔ The best way to show someone you love them is physical.

Challenge everyone to be aware of hidden influences, and point out how, even in the activity you have just done, the pressure to be like everyone else influences us. One day we will meet Jesus in person and he will ask us, not about money, fashion, sex or behaviour, but about our love for him.

APPROACH 3: *CHALLENGER*

1 DISCUSSION (15 minutes)
Split the teenagers into subgroups of three or four and give each subgroup a copy of the mock newspapers *The Misinformer* and *The Smut* photocopied from page 43. Display the following instructions and questions for the subgroups to work on.

1 Match up the same stories in the two newspapers, joining the headlines with a pencil line.

2 What differences of approach do the pairs of headlines show?

3 What assumptions lie behind the headlines about:

- money
- sex
- politics
- fashion
- Britain
- teenagers

4 Is this activity fair on newspapers? Are the joke titles justified? Are there really hidden influences like this in society and the media? Have you ever been influenced in a way you now regret (eg bought something you'll never wear again)?

2 TALK (5 minutes)
Make these points:

■ *Your mind is precious. That's why people are after it! Most of the things that influence us are not on the surface, but hidden.*

■ *FOR EXAMPLE, a newspaper reports two muggings. The first is reported, 'Two youths attacked ...'. The second is reported, 'Two black youths attacked ...'. Why did the second report* draw attention to the race of the criminals, while the first (in which the criminals were white) did not? Probably just bad journalism, but the result is that a completely unfair impression of blacks slips into people's minds. And God, who is a black God as well as a white God, hates the hidden influence of racism.

■ *ANOTHER TRUE EXAMPLE: In 1989 a man won £1.5 million on the pools. The tabloid newspapers reported it, and next day ran a headline about the girl who turned down a marriage proposal from the man two months before. 'The unluckiest girl in the world' was the headline. The assumption was that the money was important, her love for the man (or lack of it) was incidental. A hidden influence, because the attitudes rub off.*

Paul recommended: 'Don't let the world around you squeeze you into its mould' (Romans 12:2, J B Phillips). Take an active role in what enters your mind, and 'let God remould your mind from within'.

Be aware that:

✔ *Advertisers may be trying to sell you something you don't want.*

✔ *Fashion changes every year because manufacturers are after your money.*

✔ *Anyone who stops you in the street to talk about life is biassed (and that includes Christians!).*

✔ *Newspapers and TV can tell the same story in different ways depending on which person they sympathise with.*

✔ *Materialism (money and possessions are most important) is definitely not the only approach to life.*

✔ *You don't have to do what everyone else in your age group is doing.*

Does this leave you asking, 'How can I know

what is true?' Pilate asked Jesus that question (John 18:38) without knowing that Jesus had already answered it (John 8:31-32). God has offered to guard our minds if we allow him to do so by staying united with Jesus (Philippians 4:7). Beware hidden influences!

3 YOUR OPINION (10 minutes)

Ask everyone to stand in the middle of the room. You are going to make some statements. If people agree totally, they stand on the right side of the room. If they disagree, they move to the left side. If they are completely undecided, they stand in the centre, but they may position themselves anywhere else in between if they veer slightly more to one opinion than the other:

✔ It is vital to have a car to drive once you are seventeen.

✔ If hot pants, flares, plus fours or bondage trousers come back into fashion, I would wear them, even if I don't know what they are!

✔ I should cut off my friendship with someone who decides to sleep with their boyfriend/girlfriend.

✔ Big prize gameshows on TV encourage materialism in a harmful way.

✔ Moral standards should be set by what the majority of the population find acceptable.

✔ Men should earn money; women should look after babies.

✔ The best way to show someone you love them is physical.

✔ I'm prepared to stand out from my friends on some issues of morality or fashion.

✔ As well as praising God and Jesus, we should worship angels.

✔ God is pleased if we keep telling people we are pathetic and they are better than us.

✔ When you have sexy thoughts, the best thing to do is beat yourself about until they go away.

4 BIBLE STUDY (20 minutes)

Invite someone to read Colossians 2:20-3:4, then ask everyone to return to their subgroups in order to discuss these questions, displayed for all to see:

? *The final three statements on which you gave your opinion were man-made rules which were influencing the church at Colossae. What would the Colossians have learnt about them from Paul?*

? *Paul sees beginning to follow Christ as 'dying' with him and 'being resurrected' with him. According to the passage, what should be the practical result of dying with Christ? What should be the practical result of being raised to life with Christ?*

? *If Paul was writing today, which of the 'rules' of our generation which 'appear to be based on wisdom' might he criticise?*

? *How can we 'keep our minds fixed on things in heaven'?*

? *Does this mean that we should completely ignore what is fashionable in clothes, music and among our friends? Is there a way of enjoying the influences of society, but still letting Jesus control our 'real lives' (v 4)?*

5 PRAYER (10 minutes)

Ask the groups to share their replies to question 3, and write up the rules for all to see. When there are several, use them as the basis for a responsive prayer. Read them out one at a time, each followed by this response:

Leader: Lord Jesus, you understand this pressure on us,
All: Guard our hearts and minds.

Follow this with a time of open prayer for your country, its values, its government, its media, and for Christians who are in a position to influence the way people think.

The Misinformer

GOVERNMENT MINISTER'S SPEECH WELL RECEIVED BY TEENS

LABOUR MAKING ADVANCES IN OVER A QUARTER OF CONSTITUENCIES

LONDON GANG CLAIMS SEVERE PROVOCATION LED THEM TO SETTING ON HOLIDAYING GROUP.

Seven Americans and a local boy in hospital.

SURVEY SHOWS 82% THINK SEX BEFORE MARRIAGE IS ACCEPTABLE

THROW AWAY THOSE TRAINERS! It's going to be leather boots this winter.

Stroll on teenagers!

£1 MILLION POOLS WINNER SAYS – 'NOW LIFE IS PERFECT'

LUCKY LINDA WINS LIBEL LOLLY

Court demands paper pays £50,000

The Smut

MINISTER SPELLS OUT GOVERNMENT POLICY ON TEENAGERS

YANKS TAUNT SCHOOLBOYS–

one Brit seriously ill

LINDA BLACK'S LIBEL CASE

AGAINST THE MISINFORMER ENDS – PAPER ADMITS LIES. SHE SAYS, 'MY LIFE IS RUINED. I MUST LEAVE THE COUNTRY.'

Millionaire's children say, 'WHY DOESN'T HE LOVE US ANY MORE?'

74% OF ELECTION SEATS LIKELY TO GO TO TORIES

Fashion and leather industries combine in massive footwear promotion

43

CHAPTER 6

PARTIES AND ALCOHOL

WHAT'S THE BIG IDEA?

Parties are a great source of pleasure for teenagers, but also a source of frustration if they lead to conflict with parents or friends. The potential freedom brings with it potential temptation. This programme gives its participants a chance to work out their attitudes to features of party-going at a time when they are not under pressure to make instant decisions. The Bible's attitude to alcohol and parties is revealed as practical wisdom, not a puritanical attempt to stifle joy. Those who are committed to living out the Bible's plan are encouraged to find cultural equivalents for our society.

PRINCIPAL BIBLE PASSAGE
EPHESIANS 5:1–20

OTHER PASSAGES USED
GENESIS 9:21, PSALM 104:15,
PROVERBS 20:1; 21:17; 23:26-35; 31:5,
ECCLESIASTES 10:19, MATTHEW 9:10-15,
LUKE 14:12-14; 17:3-4, JOHN 2:3-10;
17:15, ROMANS 12:2; 14:13-15,
1 CORINTHIANS 6:19-20; 11:25,
GALATIANS 5:13-15, 1 TIMOTHY 5:23

RESOURCES
ALCOHOLICS ANONYMOUS, PO BOX 1,
STONEBOW HOUSE, STONEBOW, YORK
YO1 2NJ (071 352 3001)
AL ATEEN, 61 GREAT DOVER STREET,
LONDON SE1 4YF (071 403 0888) – FOR
TEENAGERS WHO HAVE A RELATIVE WITH
A DRINK PROBLEM
BAND OF HOPE, FREEPOST, LONDON
SW1P 3YY
'DRUGS AND YOU', GRAHAME KNOX,
KINGSWAY

MAJOR POINTS THAT CAN BE MADE

♦ Jesus enjoyed socialising, but saw celebrations as a way of building each other up, not an excuse for selfish or immoral pleasure.

♦ Many features of today's parties are not mentioned in the Bible, but its principles of taking care to be distinctive as Christians, and not allowing our bodies to be damaged, throw light on them. It is the responsibility of each person to make decisions in a godly way about how to enjoy life without excess.

♦ As an example, alcohol was created as a good and pleasurable thing, but its misuse can hurt us, hurt those we know, and shame God. There *is* a wise approach to alcohol, but not everyone agrees on what that means.

♦ Temptations run high at parties. Make your mind up *before* you go what God wants you to do when you are there.

APPROACH 1: INVESTIGATOR

1 WHAT'S IN A PARTY?
(10 minutes)

Split the gathering into small groups. Give each group a cardboard tube, scissors, paste, crepe or foil paper, a pencil and a strip of self-adhesive labels. On the labels they write all the things they can think of that are available at parties of any kind – one on each. The list will include such things as alcohol, cigarettes, dancing, kissograms, games, company, conversation, snogging, food, jokes, fancy dress, things getting broken, soft porn videos, parents getting strife and so on. It can obviously be longer than that. They put the slips of paper inside the tube, and around it make a party cracker.

2 DISCUSSION AND DECISION (30 minutes)

The groups then each give their cracker to another group. They are also given a large piece of white paper, a red piece, and a piece in a murky colour. They are to pull their new cracker and take the labels out. They must decide where they fit in each of three categories:

✔ Those which they think God would take delight in – these they attach to the white sheet.

✔ Those which God would forbid – these they attach to the red sheet.

✔ Those which are not wrong in themselves but are open to abuse - these they attach to the sheet of indeterminate colour.

When this is complete, they display their conclusions, and wander round to look at the others. Bring them together as a large group for discussion. The leader should also have looked at the displays and may want to challenge them if some things are missing - for instance, are drugs on the list even if they do not feature in the parties that the teenagers present go to? Have they included hassle over what time parents want them home? Were they realistic over drunkenness and its results? Is driving after drinking alcohol on the list? It should be. Turn your attention to the features they have placed on the murky sheet of paper. Hold a discussion which includes these points:

❏ Were people surprised at where the group that received their cracker put any of the slips which they had prepared?

❏ Go through the elements which are open to abuse one at a time, asking at what point they cease to be joyful and start to be damaging. Allow those present freely to disagree with each other.

3 BIBLE STUDY (10 minutes)

Ask the group to split into their subgroups again. Give each subgroup a photocopy of the sheet 'Alcohol: whose problem?' from page 49, and invite them to work through it together. Afterwards, ask them to share with others the practical advice for the twentieth century they added to the lists.

4 TALK (5 minutes)
Make these points:

❏ Jesus enjoyed socialising. He didn't only go to parties attended by 'religious' people – he mixed with all sorts. When asked why he didn't go out of his way to avoid pleasures like these, he replied: 'Why should people be sad when I'm around – it's like being miserable at a wedding reception. It's life *without* me that is dull' (Matthew 9:10-15).

❏ However, our bodies are a gift from God and it is his intention that the Holy Spirit should 'dwell' within them. We are to use our bodies in a way which pleases God. Nearly all the warnings against drunkenness and excess in the Bible are for *practical* reasons. We are not to damage ourselves (1 Corinthians 6:19-20).

❏ If the Holy Spirit is in control of our lives, we can find approaches to alcohol and all the other joyful features of parties so as to build up both others and ourselves, without hurting our relationship with God. The Bible says that getting close to God through the Holy Spirit makes a party look like a non-event (Ephesians 5:15–18)!

5 PRAYER (5 minutes)
On the back of the sheet, invite everyone present to write their personal opinion about:

●◆ *The best thing about a good party.*

●◆ *The worst thing about a boring party.*

●◆ *The easiest way to get carried away at a party and do something you will regret.*

Ask them to mark those three things according to how much joy they think God takes in them, from five stars to none at all. The leader should then pray that they will have parties where all the stars come out!

APPROACH 2: *PIONEER*

1 *MAKE YOUR MIND UP*
(7 minutes)

Give each person a handful of matchsticks and paper clips. Lay out a line of bowls, each labelled to represent something that has been known to happen at a party. The members of the group should put either a matchstick or a paper clip in each bowl. A matchstick means: 'This is stupid'. A paper clip means: 'This is cool'. After votes have been cast, announce whether there are more matchsticks or paper clips in each bowl. The bowls say:

2 *TALK* (3 minutes)
Make these points:

❗ There are loads of references to parties in the Bible. Jesus enjoyed socialising – there are over a dozen mentions of him going to a party.

❗ God intended that celebrations should be enjoyable - in fact Jesus reacted against people who criticised him for feasting. He never forbade alcohol either - it can be a good thing.

❗ However, there are some specific warnings in the Bible, particularly in a collection of wise sayings called Proverbs: 'Drinking too much makes you loud and foolish. It's stupid to get drunk ... Don't let them spike your drinks or you'll wake up feeling like a snake has bitten you ... Don't go to a party looking for easy sex.'

❗ Parties were created good; parties are dangerous! Alcohol was created good; alcohol is dangerous! Be wise!

(Proverbs 20:1; 23:26-35, Matthew 9:10-15, John 2:3-10)

STAY UP ALL NIGHT AND SKIP GOING TO BED.

THROW UP.

PLAY GAMES.

DELIBERATELY STAY OUT LATER THAN YOUR PARENTS SAY.

REFUSE TO DANCE BECAUSE IT'S STUPID.

SET OUT TO FIND SOMEONE TO GET OFF WITH.

ACCEPT DRUGS.

REFUSE TO GO TO PARTIES FOR RELIGIOUS REASONS.

DRIVE HOME AFTER DRINKING ANY ALCOHOL AT ALL.

DANCE OR FLIRT WITH SOMEONE ELSE'S GIRL/BOY.

DRIVE HOME AFTER DRINKING MORE THAN THE LEGAL LIMIT.

SEND A KISSOGRAM.

CRASH A PARTY YOU WEREN'T INVITED TO.

GET DRUNK.

TAKE OFF YOUR CLOTHES.

APPROACH 3: *CHALLENGER*

1 *ONCE-IN-A-LIFETIME*
(10 minutes)

Give out photocopies of the sheet 'Plan a party' (page 50). The groups are to get into pairs and, between them, plan the best party they can imagine. Money is no problem.

2 *DISCUSSION* (20 minutes)
Ask each pair to tell the rest of the group what they decided in the categories 'The thing that would trouble my morals most' and 'The worst thing that could happen'. Write them up as two lists. The leader may feel that it is right to add some other 'danger points' which may possibly feature in parties to which members

of the group are invited. Consider, for instance, adding: drinks getting spiked, gatecrashing, loud music keeping neighbours awake late at night, friends getting off with someone else's girl/boy, strippers being hired as a joke, soft porn videos, drunkenness and so on. Do not use this as a way of over-riding the teenagers' suggestions, but make sure that important issues are not overlooked.

Split the group into subgroups of three or four. Read them six Bible principles from Luke 17:3-4, Romans 12:2; 14:13-15, 1 Corinthians 6:19-20, Galatians 5:13-15, Ephesians 5:15-18. Display the references so that they can look them up again in Bibles. Divide the items on the list of party features so that each subgroup has two or three to discuss. Pose the question: 'What would/will you do in order to serve Jesus effectively at a party where this was happening?' They are to answer the question in the light of the Bible references. After a few minutes, ask each group to report what they decided, and open the issues for discussion.

3 PRAYER (5 minutes)
Hold a time of open prayer. First, thank God for all the good things involved in parties. Second, ask God for wisdom and strength of character to do what is right when parties bring moral dilemmas.

4 TALK (5 minutes)
Make these points:

✔ Jesus enjoyed socialising, and didn't only go to parties given by 'religious' people (Matthew 9:10-15).

✔ He assumed that his followers would celebrate, but he wanted to see those times transformed from ones which are selfishly motivated into events which are generous toward the lonely, the poor and those in need (Luke 14:12-14).

✔ We are not to address the moral problems that parties bring by refusing ever to go. We are called to take part, to make it clear that we will not do what is wrong, and to be good influences. Jesus doesn't want us taken out of the 'the world', but protected from it (John 17:15).

✔ Sometimes it will be appropriate to take a

stronger stand than others. Hence the discussion about what to do in certain situations. Only the wisdom of the Holy Spirit can show us what to say about the Bible's standards and when to say it. That comes from experience and encountering him in prayer (Ephesians 5:15-18).

5 BIBLE STUDY (10 minutes)
As a practical exploration of one of the problem areas, give each subgroup a photocopy of the sheet 'Alcohol: whose problem?' from page 49, and invite the teenagers to work through it together.

6 MAKING DECISIONS (10 minutes)
There are many ways for those throwing parties to face the alcohol dilemma. Which is best? Around the walls, post sheets of paper, each bearing one of the following pieces of advice. Each person present should take a pencil and go round reading every sheet. They may give marks – 0, 1, 2, 3 – depending on how good they think that way of facing the problem is. They indicate this by putting ticks on the paper.

✔ HAVE NO ALCOHOL AT ALL AT THE PARTY

✔ ALWAYS PROVIDE INTERESTING NON-ALCOHOLIC ALTERNATIVES AS WELL AS ALCOHOL

✔ ASK AN ADULT TO SERVE ALL THE DRINKS AND KEEP AN EYE ON WHAT HAPPENS

✔ PROVIDE ONLY LOW-ALCOHOL BEER AND WINE

✔ BAN SPIRITS

✔ ASK SEVERAL CAR-DRIVERS TO STAY OFF ALCOHOL AND OFFER LIFTS HOME TO ANYONE WHO MAY BE OVER THE LIMIT

✔ ON THE INVITATIONS ASK SOME OF THE GUESTS, 'PLEASE BRING A NON-ALCOHOLIC BOTTLE'

✔ PROVIDE ALCOHOL AND TRUST THE JUDGMENT OF YOUR FRIENDS

✔ DON'T PUT ALL THE BOTTLES AND CANS OUT AT ONE GO

When everyone has finished, tot up a total

score for each and announce what has emerged as the collective wisdom of the group. Close the session by praying for teenagers who are addicted to alcohol, those whose only reason for going to parties is to get drunk, those who are suffering because of drunk drivers, and those who are seriously trying to dry out.

DO YOU AGREE OR DISAGREE?

Always provide interesting non-alcoholic alternatives as well as alcohol.

DO YOU AGREE OR DISAGREE?

HAVE NO ALCOHOL AT ALL AT THE PARTY.

DO YOU AGREE OR DISAGREE?

ASK AN ADULT TO SERVE ALL THE DRINKS AND KEEP AN EYE ON WHAT HAPPENS.

DO YOU AGREE OR DISAGREE?

Provide only low-alcohol beer and wine.

DO YOU AGREE OR DISAGREE?

BAN SPIRITS.

DO YOU AGREE OR DISAGREE?

PROVIDE ALCOHOL AND TRUST THE JUDGMENT OF YOUR FRIENDS.

DO YOU AGREE OR DISAGREE?

Ask several car drivers to stay off alcohol and offer lifts home to anyone who may be over the limit.

DO YOU AGREE OR DISAGREE?

DON'T PUT ALL THE BOTTLES AND CANS OUT AT ONE GO.

DO YOU AGREE OR DISAGREE?

On the invitations ask some of the guests, 'Please bring a non-alcoholic bottle'.

ALCOHOL
WHOSE PROBLEM?

The Bible says many practical things about drink - it nearly always refers to wine, because beer and spirits were not so common then. Read these sentences and find in them the good things the Bible says about alcohol and the bad results it warns of.

GOOD THINGS

"When they drink, they forget the laws and ignore the rights of people in need."
PROVERBS 31:5

Indulging in wine ... will never make you wealthy.
PROVERBS 21:17

Take a little wine to help your digestion, since you are ill so often.
1 TIMOTHY 5:28

"After supper Jesus took the cup and said ... 'Whenever you drink it, do so in memory of me.'"
1 CORINTHIANS 11:25

After he drank some of the wine, he became drunk and took off his clothes. GENESIS 9:21

BAD THINGS

The next morning you will feel like you have been bitten by a poisonous snake. You will not be able to think or speak clearly ... you will say, 'I must have been beaten up.'
PROVERBS 23:32-33

You produce wine to make us happy.
PSALM 104:15

"Drinking too much makes you loud and foolish. It's stupid to get drunk."
PROVERBS 20:1

"Feasting makes you happy and wine cheers you up, but you can't have either without money."
ECCLESIASTES 10:19

Are you surprised by any of these?
All these sentences were written thousands of years ago. Decide with your group on one good practical thing about alcohol and one bad practical thing about it which the Bible might say if it were being written now at the end of the twentieth century. Add them to the lists.

PLAN A PARTY!

This is your perfect party - money is no problem!

The food and drink I would serve are

The best thing that could happen is...

The theme or decorations I would have are

The thing that would trouble my morals most if it happened is

The worst thing that could happen is

This is the music/entertainment I would have

CHAPTER 7

CINEMA, TV AND MUSIC

WHAT'S THE BIG IDEA?

This programme is based on the assumption that creativity is good and godly, although it has been abused. It asks teenagers to consider that there is more to entertainment than meets the eye, and that even trivial pop songs have values behind them which may or may not measure favourably against God's standards. Making the assumption that avoiding entertainment altogether is neither possible nor desirable, teenagers are invited to work out their criteria for what is right to watch and listen to, whether or not their attitude to God brings his standards into their decision-making. Those who want to worship God are invited to use their God-given creativity to do so.

PRINCIPAL BIBLE PASSAGE
PHILIPPIANS 4:7-9

MAJOR POINTS THAT CAN BE MADE

◆ It is only because God is a creator that humans, made in his image, can be creative. The arts are good!

◆ Entertainment is also open to abuse, like every other part of creation, and Christians are called to be selective about what their minds dwell on.

OTHER PASSAGES USED
GENESIS 1:26, EXODUS 14:21-25;
15:19-21; 32:1-20, PSALM 87:7; 149:1-5;
150:1-6, ISAIAH 20:1-4, JEREMIAH 27:1-2;
28:10-14; 31:1-4, MATTHEW 14:1-11

◆ It is no good making bald statements about rock music, dancing, violence in art and so on. The issues are complex and we need to be open to God controlling the way we decide what to see and hear.

◆ Whatever show you go to, you are effectively taking Jesus to it with you. Is he having as good a time as you?

APPROACH 1: INVESTIGATOR

1 PLAN YOUR VIEWING
(10 minutes)

Split the gathering into subgroups and give each one a photocopy of the sheet 'On the box!' from page 56. Between them, they are to plan four hours worth of viewing. They may specify either types of programme (eg a snooker match), or a named programme (eg Coronation Street), or a type of film (which may be assumed to last 90 minutes). The selection may contain up to six items, but it must be agreed by the whole subgroup and contain something to please each of them.

RESOURCES
'THE TIME OF YOUR LIFE', ALAN
MACDONALD, FRAMEWORKS

On the television screen, they are to represent their six chosen programmes with drawings and titles.

2 MEASURING UP
(10 minutes)

Refer them to the lower part of the sheet. The subgroups are to judge the value of the six programmes they have chosen in each of four categories:

ENTERTAINMENT (How enjoyable is it to watch?)

 # PRODUCTION VALUES (Is it well presented, written, acted designed etc?)

 # CONTENT (Are there things in it to provoke thought or is it mindless?)

 # WORTH (Can you be a better person as a result of seeing it?)

They may give up to ten decibels on the volume chart for each programme, by shading in the boxes appropriately. Again, they must reach a joint decision.

When they have completed this, challenge them as to whether they have devised a balanced programme of viewing. Is there enough in it of lasting value? Is there too much or too little straightforward fun? Ask them briefly to discuss this in their subgroups.

3 TALK (5 minutes)
Make these points:

◆ *God made humans to be creative, and his attitude is that arts and entertainment are good and there to be enjoyed, both as audience and performers (Psalm 87:7).*

◆ *Like everything else in creation, entertainment is now open to abuse as well as godly use. Rather than just let music, films or TV flow over us, God asks us to think about what we should watch and listen to. He doesn't ban everything except 'Songs of Praise' and 'Chariots of fire', but he does set us standards (Philippians 4:8). There is a reason for it – he wants to keep our hearts and minds peaceful and safe (Philippians 4:7).*

◆ *Try the 'Acid Granny' test – would you enjoy this in the same way if Jesus was sitting next to you? Christians will always disagree as to what is acceptable and what is not. Just be sure that you are making up your own mind, rather than letting entertainment shape you without you realising it.*

4 HOW DO YOU DECIDE?
(10 minutes)

Give each subgroup six self-adhesive address labels and the sheet 'How do you decide?', photocopied from page 57. Ask them to divide each label into eight. Read Philippians 4:8 to them and ask them to write one of the items on this checklist in each of the eight spaces:

☐ GOOD   ☐ DESERVES PRAISE
☐ TRUE   ☐ NOBLE
☐ RIGHT   ☐ PURE
☐ LOVELY   ☐ HONOURABLE

They do this six times and cut up the labels.

They are to read the six scenarios printed on the television screens. In each case they decide whether any of the eight qualities on their labels can be applied to the scene described. If it can, they peel off the label and stick it on the picture. They must try to reach a joint decision. Point out that members of the groups might genuinely disagree about the acceptability of all the scenes illustrated.

5 DISCUSSION (20 minutes)
Bring the whole group together for a discussion. It may be helpful to use the scenarios the group have just discussed as examples, but make sure you also bring features of current films, the rock charts and television into the discussion. Here are some questions which may open the possibilities of the discussion:

? *Is it reasonable to let God take control of your attitude to entertainment, or is what you do in your 'happy hour' your own business?*

? *Violence is always controversial in entertainment. Are there occasions when violence can be used with good intentions on television? How do you tell the difference between those occasions and video nasties which make money out of human's worst instincts, such as enjoying seeing people suffer? Should there be safeguards to protect certain people, eg children?*

? *Most of us have the radio on for long stretches and hear a heap of music, some good, some bad, some with a message that goes against what Christians believe. Can this influence the way we think? Does it matter that we listen to songs with a non-Christian point of view?*

? *Most 15 certificate films and many late evening telly programmes show sex scenes of some kind. They rarely portray a man and woman married to each other, which is the only kind of sex God delights in. Does it matter to see naked people in a film? Does it matter to see kinds of sex which Christians believe to be wrong? Are those two questions the same?*

? *Surely just because you watch or listen to a non-Christian point of view, it doesn't mean you agree with it. True?*

? *Is it possible to watch too much TV or listen to too much pop?*

6 PRAYER AND REACTION (5 minutes)

Give each person a cocktail stick or matchstick. Ask them to prepare themselves by thinking of their favourite film, television programme and record. Ask them in silence to do the 'Acid Granny' test and decide whether they can thank God with sincerity for the joy that item of entertainment brings.

Use this prayer, everyone shouting the reply together and inserting their personal favourites in the gaps.

> **Leader:** Thank you, Lord, for cinema.
> **All:** Thank you, Lord, for ....
> **Leader:** Thank you, Lord, for television.
> **All:** Thank you, Lord, for ....
> **Leader:** Thank you, Lord, for music.
> **All:** Thank you, Lord, for ....

Place a jar by the door and invite people to make a specific reaction to what they have been thinking about during the session. Suggest that they put their cocktail stick in the jar as they leave. If they put it in broken, it means: 'I am prepared to let God be part of my decisions about what to watch and listen to.' If it is unbroken: 'No change.' This is to be an 'acted out' sign between them and God.

APPROACH 2: PIONEER

1 YOU CHOOSE (6 minutes)

Give each person twenty dried peas (or something similar). On a table, lay out fifteen bowls, each labelled with one of the following: Good jokes, action, music score, hype, love scenes, costumes and scenery, good acting, blood and guts, beautiful to look at, being with the right girl/boy, makes you think about important things, famous stars in it, T-shirt/poster/baseball-cap that you can buy with it, being frightened, emotional ending.

Pose the question: 'What makes a really good film?' Everyone is allowed to vote by putting peas in the relevant bowls. They can give more than one vote to particular categories (although they are not allowed to 'flood' any one bowl as a joke), and some of them may not warrant any votes at all. If someone suggests an additional feature, put out another bowl and label it accordingly.

When everyone has used their votes, add up the results (involve the group members in counting and writing up the score). Declare what the collective opinion of the group has turned out to be. Suggest that God has an opinion about entertainment too. It is not one that he wants to force on us, but since he created all the technology and imagination involved in entertainment, it is worth taking his opinion seriously.

2 TALK (4 minutes)

Make these points:

◆ God is a brilliant creator. He created humans, and he made us like him in many ways. One way is that humans too have a desire to create; to create what is good.

◆ Dance, music and entertainment have always been part of the life of God's people. Whole books of the Bible are songs! God's messengers (prophets) often acted his messages as drama. If the Bible writers were alive today, they would certainly use all kinds of entertainment forms that are available to us. Like everything else, entertainment is open to abuse as well as to godly use. Today, therefore, when something is creative it isn't necessarily always good.

◆ God says, 'Don't just watch or listen to any old thing. Think first!' God's good gift has been exploited by people who want to make a load of money and are prepared to bring out the worst in humans, such as their enjoyment of seeing others suffer.

◆ Christians differ over what is right to watch or listen to, and what is wrong. You have to make up *your own* mind. Think about God's point of view before you allow a money-grabber to bring out the worst in you.

(Genesis 1:26, Psalm 87:7, Philippians 4:8-9)

APPROACH 3: *CHALLENGER*

1 TALK (5 minutes)
Make these points:

♦ Creativity is part of God's nature. Because we are made in God's image, humans too have built into them by God the ability and desire to create things artistically. The psalms teach entertainers to see their artistry as God-given: 'All my springs are in you.' (Genesis 1:26, Psalm 87:7).

♦ Sin entered art and entertainment, just like it entered everything else in God's creation, so it is now open to abuse as well as to godly use. The Old Testament prophets used drama to bring God's message in a godly way. For instance, Jeremiah put on an ox yoke in his play warning Israel that they would be yoked into working for the enemy Babylon (Jeremiah 27:1-2; 28:10-14). Isaiah even did a nude scene in his anxiety to show Israel the danger that their land would be stripped bare by Assyria (Isaiah 20:1-4, which probably means that he wore only a loincloth).

♦ We realise that not everything in film, television or music is good for us. Philippians 4:8 may help us decide what to listen to or what to avoid seeing. It still leaves difficulties. An anti-war film may have a violent scene which is nevertheless 'true' and 'honourable'. A romantic or sex scene on TV may be 'lovely', but gives the impression that promiscuity is an acceptable way of life. A rock album may 'deserve praise' but promote money-is-everything values. But, equally, a worship tape may be so shoddily put together that it doesn't 'deserve praise' at all.

Some suggested ground rules:

- Don't break the law (eg, certificates on hired videos).
- Go for entertainment that will bring out the best in you, so you don't have to pretend you enjoyed something you didn't.
- Be prepared to switch off, walk out, turn the volume down, phone and complain, phone and congratulate, scream for more, cut down, or cut out – when appropriate.
- Give Jesus a good time at the shows you are taking him to.

2 BIBLE STUDY (15 minutes)
Point out that the means of entertainment available to us have dramatically increased since the Bible was written. To find out what the Bible wants us to think about video, comics, films and so on, we need to unearth the principles behind its attitude to entertainment and carry them forward to apply to our society. The Bible study focuses on one form of entertainment which was as popular then as now – dancing.

Split the group into subgroups and ask them to read five Bible passages – Exodus 14:21-25 and 15:19-21, Exodus 32:1-20, Psalm 149:1-5, Jeremiah 31:1-4, Matthew 14:1-11. Then invite them to discuss these questions.

1. ***On which of these occasions would God take delight in the dancing and on which would it sadden him? How do you decide?***
2. ***What principles emerge about times when dancing is welcome and times when it is abused?***
3. ***Think of two situations in today's scene; one where dancing or watching dancing would please God, and one where it would offend him.***
4. ***Think of one entertainment form not mentioned in the Bible. Invent two situations – one where it would please God and one where the form is being abused.***

After some time, invite the subgroups to share with each other the forms of entertainment they thought of for question 4.

3 DEBATE (15 minutes)
In advance of the meeting, invite two members of the group each to prepare a two-minute speech to represent views about how to respond to the dilemma. It is preferable to invite people who actually hold these views, but there is no reason why this should necessarily be the case.

The first one argues that we should only listen to Christian music and watch Christian programmes. He or she might point out that the arts have been hijacked by people who are anti-Christian or out to make money regardless of standards (give examples). Sex, violence and bad language have become commonplace on television even when they are irrelevant to the subject. They subconsciously lead us away from Christ. To stay pure we must only experience concerts, plays, records, films and so on which are dedicated to glorifying God.

The second one argues that we are quite free to enjoy entertainment created by non-Christians, but we must judge each case by its merits. God gave his gift of creativity to all people, not just to Christians. There are some records and programmes by non-Christians which, although not specifically Christian, benefit humankind and make our lives better (give examples). There are even occasions when violence and romantic scenes can be used in a good way, because they make people realise what is moral and what they must reject. The solution is to think before we see or hear something, then experience what we think Jesus would be content for us to experience.

After the speeches, open the debate into a discussion, to which all may contribute, on how to decide what forms of entertainment are right for us to attend and how we should make up our minds as to what is acceptable and what we should walk out of.

4 CREATIVE WORSHIP
(25 minutes)

Ask those present to return to their subgroups to devise a means of worshipping God. Explain that what they create should be entertaining, and also honouring to God. Refer them to Psalm 150, which is to be the basis of their worship. They may use any art-form to interpret it, and some suggestions appear below. The leader should decide which approaches are viable and provide appropriate materials and equipment for the groups to choose from:

DANCE. Devise a set of steps to the song 'Praise him on the trumpet', based on this psalm, published in Songs of Fellowship 2 *and* Mission Praise 2, *among others, and recorded on many worship tapes. They may either sing the song themselves or move using a cassette as an accompaniment. Alternatively, provide a range of instrumental cassettes and invite them to make their own choice of song to which to dance.*

ART. Create a collage or banner using drawings, materials or magazine photographs, which expresses the theme of the psalm.

POETRY. Compose a rap, expressing words which are inspired by those in the psalm. They should be chanted over a background of finger-clicking, clapping or a drum machine.

MUSIC. Compose a song, using a well-known tune, such as a TV theme-song. Write words which reflect those in the psalm to fit the tune.

RADIO. Arrange a choral reading of Psalm 150, with a variety of readers and sound effects. Record it on to a cassette or perform it live.

FILM. Use a video camera to film sights which inspire praise of God with the psalm as a commentary, or make a film of the choral reading described above.

DRAMA. Write a sketch in which all the characters are instruments of an orchestra. Some feel they are not allowed to praise God because they are too noisy, too insignificant and so on. Alternatively, a sketch in which 'Disgusted of Tunbridge Wells' is appalled at the idea that anything entertaining or joyful is allowable as a Christian until someone directs him or her to this psalm, with astonishing consequences!

CABARET. Identify a hidden talent in every one of the subgroup, such as ear-wiggling, juggling, going cross-eyed, turning cartwheels, playing the spoons, belching at will. Present a new psalm, based on the structure of Psalm 150, allowing each person to contribute their speciality: 'Praise him with the juggling, praise him with the comb-and-paper playing', and so on.

When the groups have had 15 minutes or more to prepare, invite them each to present their act of worship for all to share. Stress that these are all meant to be entertaining, because God is the God of creativity. However, despite the laughter, they are also intended to be serious acts of worship, not just excuses for someone to show off.

Afterwards, all read the psalm through in its published form as a united, closing act of praise.

ON THE BOX!

HOW WOULD YOU RATE THE PROGRAMMES YOU CHOOSE TO WATCH?

ENTERTAINMENT — How enjoyable is it to watch?

PRODUCTION VALUES — Is it well presented, written, acted, designed, etc?

CONTENT — Are there things in it to provoke thought or is it mindless?

WORTH — Can you be a better person as a result of seeing it?

N A M E	N A M E	N A M E	N A M E	N A M E	N A M E

ENTERTAINMENT PRODUCTION VALUES CONTENT WORTH

ENTERTAINMENT PRODUCTION VALUES CONTENT WORTH

ENTERTAINMENT PRODUCTION VALUES CONTENT WORTH

ENTERTAINMENT PRODUCTION VALUES CONTENT WORTH

ENTERTAINMENT PRODUCTION VALUES CONTENT WORTH

ENTERTAINMENT PRODUCTION VALUES CONTENT WORTH

HOW DO YOU DECIDE?

■ **TEENIE BOPSALONG,** the new Australian sensation, bounces on stage and her audience scream. You can only just hear her catchy, million-selling hit lyric. Joy erupts all round the stadium at the squeaky-clean marvel, whose dance routine is as flawless as her complexion:

If only you would love me
    nothing else would
    matter,
Holding you just makes me
    wanna sing,
Got no time to think about
    the world and all its
    problems,
Kissing you's the most
    important thing.

■ **BARRY MUGGING** was coming to the end of his hilarious set at the Palladium. No one was safe from his targets! Everyone roared as mothers-in-law, Irishmen, gays, Muslims and nuns could all have a good laugh at each other. The contented audience smiled their way home. 'Isn't it refreshing,' said one woman to another, 'to have a whole evening with no vulgar jokes and not a single swear-word.'

■ To the chords of the year's best-selling love song, the movie reaches its final scene. **MICHELLE** has refused to believe Lee was dead and she has fended off a knife-killer, despair and several attempts to seduce her. Faithful to the man she loves, she lies beside him in their honeymoon suite. 'You waited for me?' he asks. She nods, and shuts her eyes as the camera follows his hand, moving from her hair gently down her spine.

■ **THE 'ZOMBIE THRASH' GIG** is coming to a close. Having been screamed at and deafened, the audience head-bang their way through the band's latest release:

Wanna hide in you,
So lonely!

Street ain't no place to make
    a home.
Don't look at the dirt, see
    the human.
Don't want your money;
    want your time.
Aaaah! Go mental! Yeah!

■ **ADAMS** picks his terrified way through the remains of a Korean village. The rain spatters on his sodden camouflage jacket. The camera makes his baby-like features look ridiculous in this uniform of war. Rapid gunfire drowns the sound of the rain and a man falls. The sergeant cries out and Adams rushes forward, teeth gritted and guns down a fleeing figure. As he approaches the corpse, you can just make out that the shot-away face was that of a young girl, perhaps twelve or thirteen. Rain trickles down the soldier's cheeks. His face says all that needs to be said – he hit the wrong target.

■ Smashing his way through the Nam jungle, **RAMBOT**, the world's first fully-robotic, fighting man-machine, reaches the settlement. This is the hero of this week's number one (Oscars for best editing, music score, costumes and make-up) film. Boy, does he slam into those gooks, blasting away with his reloading machine guns, heroically rescuing ten American citizens previously thought dead. The kids in the cinema surge with emotion at the national anthem, playing while the human-machine strides through the corpses, mercifully free of blood or mutilation.

GOD BREAKS IN

WHAT'S THE BIG IDEA?

This is deliberately a programme with less emphasis on teaching. For those with a thorough knowledge of the Christmas story it majors on worship. For those whose commitment to the meaning of Christmas is less definite, the emphasis is on fun. In all cases, the facts of the Christmas story are reiterated, but the teaching element seeks to go beyond the largely familiar narratives and explore the meaning of incarnation.

PRINCIPAL BIBLE PASSAGE
1 JOHN 1:1-7

MAJOR POINTS THAT CAN BE MADE

◆ Incarnation is the technical word for God being born in human form on Earth.

◆ Jesus was a completely human baby, but also completely God.

OTHER PASSAGES USED
NUMBERS 24:16-17, ISAIAH 9:2-7,
JEREMIAH 23:5-6, MICAH 5:2-5,
MATTHEW 1:18-24; 2:1-21, LUKE 2:1-20,
JOHN 1:1-5, 10-14, PHILIPPIANS 2:6-8,
COLOSSIANS 1:15,19, HEBREWS 1:1-3;
4:14-15

◆ It is impossible fully to understand what God is like. However, because Jesus has lived on Earth we have experienced God in a form we can understand. If we want to know: 'What is God like?' we find help by asking: 'What was Jesus like?'

◆ The key to Christmas is the name the angel gave to Jesus: 'Emmanuel'. It means 'God is with us'.

APPROACH 1: *INVESTIGATOR*

1 OUTBURST (5 minutes)

Play a version of the commercially produced game 'Outburst'. Divide the gathering into two teams. The first team is told: 'Shout out ten things about ... the wise men.' They are given 30 seconds to shout out whatever comes into their mind. Their aim is to think of everything on the following list, and their score is the number they thought of in the time. The leader says yes or no to each suggestion:

RESOURCES
'WHAT'S THE POINT OF CHRISTMAS?',
J JOHN, LION

Star	Bethlehem
The East	Herod
Gold	Frankincense
Myrrh	Worship
Children killed	Dream

The next team is told: 'Shout out ten things about ... the birth of Jesus.' The list contains:

Gabriel	Manger
Census	Angels
Shepherds	
Strips of cloth (swaddling clothes)	
Bethlehem	Mary
Joseph	Praise

At this point, fill in the gaps in the group's answers by reminding them where those they missed feature in the story. Go back to the first team for 'Ten things ... you would eat or drink at Christmas':

Turkey	Christmas pudding
Cranberry sauce	Mince pies
Brandy butter	Tangerines
Brussels sprouts	Christmas cake
Mulled wine	Stuffing

The second team has 'Ten things ... you would decorate a Christmas room with':

Tree	Cards
Tinsel	Crib
Holly	Mistletoe
Paper chains	Balloons
Candles	Lights

2 BIBLE SEARCH (10 minutes)

As a 'fun' approach to Bible study for Christmas, give out photocopies of the sheet 'Christmas crossword' (page 64), one per pair. Invite them to solve the crossword, and have available some Bibles (or photocopies of the relevant passages) in case they get stuck. Point out that the shaded letters make a word which is special to Christians at Christmas.

3 TALK (5 minutes)

Make these points:

♦ People celebrate Christmas for various reasons. The reason that Christians celebrate is that when Jesus was born in poverty and squalor it was not an ordinary birth of a baby.

♦ In some respects it was! Jesus was in every sense a human baby – crying, feeding, burping, sleeping. In another respect it was extraordinary, for God himself was being born on Earth. This is called 'incarnation'. (John 1:14 – 'the Word' is the name John uses for Jesus, before and during his life on Earth.)

♦ Why did he do this? Firstly, so that humans could understand what God was like. God is so utterly holy and unworldly that we can never understand him fully – but Jesus was God in a form that people could touch, listen to and try to understand (1 John 1:1-3).

♦ Second, and incredibly, it was so that God could become a servant to humankind, as well as its Lord (Philippians 2:6-8). We can pray to Jesus about every human feeling – disappointment, excitement, loneliness, sexuality, everything – because he knows about it from experience (Hebrews 4:14-15).

♦ It is not enough at Christmas to feel sentimental about a lovely baby in a manger. This was the day when God stepped on to Earth. It is the world's most significant day.

4 MAKING PRESENTS (20 minutes)

Remind the group that the giving of presents at Christmas is a reflection of the gifts the wise men gave to Jesus. The giving was part of their worship. Make some presents to give to special people.

You will need a tangerine (or clementine or similar fruit) per person; castor sugar, eggs, forks, bowls and grease-proof paper per group of four or five. Separate the egg and beat the white in the bowl until it is stiff. Put the castor sugar in another bowl. Break the tangerine into segments. Dip the pieces first in the egg white and then in the sugar. Place them on the grease-proof paper until the coating hardens. Polystyrene trays, decorated with tinsel and holly leaves then covered with clingfilm, could additionally be made to place the sweets in.

5 WORSHIP (20 minutes)

Give Jesus a present by giving him the pleasure of worship. Begin with the room in darkness and light a single candle. Someone should read John 1:1-5. Then everyone lights a candle of their own from the central candle.

Sing a traditional carol, and continue to alternate readings and carols by candle-light. The readings that should be used are, in this order, Matthew 1:18-24, Luke 2:1-7, Luke 2:8-20, Matthew 2:1-21. Use this prayer:

Leader: Eternal God, yet born a human baby. God has stepped into our world ...
All: Jesus we praise and adore you.
Leader: Robed in heavenly glory, yet wrapped in strips of cloth. God has stepped into our world ...
All: Jesus we praise and adore you.
Leader: Lord of heaven and earth, yet laid in a borrowed manger. God has stepped into our world ...
All: Jesus we praise and adore you.
Leader: Light of all the universe, yet born in the darkness of a stable. God has stepped into our world ...
All: Jesus we praise and adore you.

Close with a reading of 1 John 1:5-7, and a hymn about Christ the light, such as 'Shine, Jesus, Shine'.

APPROACH 2: *PIONEER*

1 *WHAT ON EARTH ...?* (5 minutes)

Ask for a volunteer to take part in an experiment. Out of sight of the rest of the group, he or she will try to describe an object so that others get an impression of what it is like. Blindfold the volunteer and produce a bowl of old-fashioned milk pudding – either tapioca or sago. First of all, the boy or girl puts his or her fingers in it and describes what it feels like (frog spawn might be the nearest comparison). The material can then be smelt, listened to and tasted. Ask whether the rest of the group felt they got an adequate impression of what the object is like. This could be repeated with a passion fruit (touch and listen to it whole, taste and smell the contents), or mozarella cheese.

Talk about how difficult it is to describe unusual things – particularly tastes. Just imagine how difficult it is to describe God – infinite, formless, utterly unworldly! You would give up a lot quicker than the tapioca taster!

2 *TALK* (3 minutes)

Make these points:

♦ It is not just difficult to describe God – it is impossible. However great we say he is, he is greater!

♦ Knowing this, God chose to come to Earth himself in a form that people could see, hear, touch, smell, taste. He came in the form of a human being – Jesus. If we want to know what God is like, we can find out what Jesus was like, for he was and is completely human and completely God.

♦ Christmas is a thrilling celebration not just because it is the birthday of a great man born in squalor and poverty in a stable, but because it is the day when God stepped on to Earth.

No wonder the whole country goes berserk that day! It's the most significant day in the history of history!

(Colossians 1:15,19, 1 John 1:1-3)

3 *WACKY GAME* (2 minutes)

Wish everyone a very happy Christmas and say that, just because Christians take Christmas seriously, it doesn't mean they don't want to have loads of fun as well. In this country, at least, they are happy to share all the traditions of a secular Christmas too.

Hang a piece of mistletoe in the middle of the room and give everyone a felt-tipped pen. They are to collect kisses in the form of felt-tip crosses on their bare feet (or perhaps their hands or knees). They have 60 seconds to collect them; they cannot receive a 'kiss' without giving one back; after being 'kissed' by one person they must collect a cross from someone else before they can have another. When time is up, declare the person with most crosses to be the winner. Take five seconds to challenge the teenagers to remember Jesus, born on earth to die on a cross and rise again to life, amid all the fun of Christmas.

APPROACH 3: *CHALLENGER*

1 *READING 1* (2 minutes)

Invite someone (with a couple of days' warning) to read Matthew 1:18-24.

2 *BIBLE STUDY* (20 minutes)

On one wall, display a simple, two-dimensional picture of a Christmas tree, cut out of green card or paper (the picture on page 63 may help you). Add some tinsel and lametta. On another wall, display this list of references:

Numbers 24:16-17	John 1:10-14
Isaiah 9:2-7	Philippians 2:6-7
Jeremiah 23:5-6	Hebrews 1:1-3
Micah 5:2-5a	1 John 1:1-3

Point out that none of these are traditional stories about Christmas. The first four were written 700 years or more before Jesus was born, and we can now see that they referred to Jesus. The New Testament passages are ones in which writers tried to explain what the significance of Jesus was. Split the group into pairs and ask them to read all the passages. After each one, they answer the question: 'How does this help us understand why Jesus was born and lived on Earth?' (You may need to explain that 'Word' means the creative wisdom of God which formed the universe, and that John used it to refer to Jesus.)

When all eight passages have been read, each pair is to choose one thing they did not previously know (or did not fully appreciate) about Jesus' birth and purpose. They should collect a small, circular piece of paper and a felt-tipped pen so that they can write their chosen fact on it. Ask one of each pair to tell the others what they chose.

3 TALK (5 minutes)
Make these points:

♦ The key to Christmas is in the name 'Emmanuel' (Matthew 1:23). It means 'God is with us'.

♦ How can we comprehend the infinite, formless, utterly holy God; perfectly loving, perfectly just? Of course, we can't! That is why Jesus came to Earth. He was and is God in a form that we can understand. Jesus was in every way a human baby – crying, feeding, burping, sleeping. He was in every way God – totally loving to his parents, completely sinless in the way he depended on them. In answer to the question, 'What is God like?', we can consider, 'What was Jesus like?' (1 John 1:1-2).

♦ In a hymn, Charles Wesley described Christmas as: 'Our God contracted to a span / Incomprehensibly made man'. The God who had everything in creation at his disposal deprived himself of everything, entering the world without even a place of his own in which to be laid (Philippians 2:7).

♦ To call Christmas a birthday underestimates it. Instead it celebrates the one and only moment in history when God stepped on to the Earth he created. Wow! The word Christians use for this is 'incarnation'.

4 PRAISE (5 minutes)
Invite one of each pair (possibly the one who did not contribute earlier) to bring their piece of circular paper and stand around the tree. One by one they read out what they have written, and then everyone says this response:

Leader: God is living with his people;
All: Jesus we praise and adore you.

While the response is being said, the person who began the prayer attaches his or her paper to the tree like a decorative bauble (use Blu-Tack).

5 READING 2 (3 minutes)
Invite a different person to read Matthew 2:1-12. At the point where the birth of Jesus is referred to, produce a small, rough packing crate stuffed with straw and slap it down in the middle of the room.

6 WORSHIP (10 minutes)
Give each person a sheet of A4 paper and ask them to divide it into four. In three of the sections, ask them to write 'gold', 'frankincense' and 'myrrh', the fourth being blank.

Talk about the three gifts of the wise men and what their significance might be interpreted as. Gold is the metal of a crown and might suggest that Jesus would be a king. Frankincense was burnt during God's worship to give off a sweet smell, and the gift speaks of Jesus both as priest and as God himself. Myrrh was an embalming resin, and Jesus' death certainly had a remarkable significance.

Three extraordinary gifts to give a baby! Ask: 'What would you have given had you gone to Bethlehem that year? That's a rhetorical question! More seriously, what will you give him this year?'

Direct the group's attention to the first section of the sheet, gold. Ask them to think what physical thing they could give to Jesus this Christmas. They are to draw it in the relevant quadrant. It might be a sum of money given to God's work, or a possession to be handed over more fully for God's use, or even something to be sold so that money is released for relief work. This might be a precious gift, like gold was to the wise man, or a simple one, but it must be realistic because God will look for these pledges to be fulfilled.

Then look at the second section, frankincense. Ask the individuals to offer as a gift to Jesus some form of service in the church, or among their friends, or in personal worship. Like incense, it is to have a spiritual *significance, not physical. They are to draw this (or write it, if it is too abstract) in the second section.*

The third section is myrrh, with its association with death. In this section they may draw something which they want to put to death in themselves so as to serve Jesus better – a habit or a bad attitude to lose. They can give it to Jesus to relieve themselves of it as part of their repentance.

In the fourth section, encourage them to draw what they would most like Jesus to present to them as a gift this Christmas.

When this is complete, they are each going to take their pledged gifts and place them in the 'manger' in the middle of the room. During this act of worship, a piece of music should be played – perhaps the carol 'In the bleak midwinter'.

7 EXCHANGE PRESENTS
(15 minutes)

Give out photocopies of the sheet 'Tree decorations' from page 63, and also some scissors and lametta. Ask everyone to cut out the two stars and fit them together by slitting them to the centre and sliding one into the other. They may colour them brightly with felt-tipped pens, then make a hole in the top and thread the lametta through, so that the three-dimensional star hangs as a decoration.

Suggest that everyone writes on the back of their decoration what they would wish for the other people in the room this Christmas. It could be a simple 'Have a happy Christmas' or a fuller statement of what God might do in the life of an individual. When everyone is ready, ask them all to swop their decoration with someone on the other side of the room, so that everyone receives one and can take it home to hang on their Christmas tree. It might be appropriate to hug the other person as they give it to him or her. They can go on swapping as often as they like as long as everyone ends with one to take home! Close by singing a familiar Christmas carol together.

TREE DECORATIONS

1. Cut along all the thick black lines.

2. Slot the two stars together.

3. Snip a tiny hole near the top, where indicated by a circle, and thread a lametta through it.

4. Write your message on the blank side, then give it to someone to hang on their Christmas tree.

CHRISTMAS CROSSWORD

1. Who told Mary that the Holy Spirit would make her pregnant? (Luke 1:26)
2. What official event made Joseph travel to Bethlehem? (Luke 2:1)
3. One of the gifts brought to Jesus by the wise men. (Matthew 2:11)
4. This king was an ancestor of Jesus. (Luke 2:4)
5. Angels told a group of shepherds not to be like this. (Luke 2:10)
6. What name of Jesus means: 'God is with us'? (Matthew 1:23)
7. What indicated to the wise men where Jesus was born? (Matthew 2:9)
8. Jesus' family fled as refugees to this country. (Matthew 2:13)
9. What did the shepherds sing to God? (Luke 2:20)
10. Who was intent on killing Jesus? (Matthew 2:13)
11. The cattle trough where Jesus was laid. (Luke 2:16)